UNIVERSITY–INDUSTRY PARTNERSHIPS FOR POSITIVE CHANGE

Transformational Strategic Alliances
Towards UN SDGs

Tim Bodley-Scott and Ersel Oymak

Foreword by
Professor Sir Anthony Finkelstein

First published in Great Britain in 2023 by

Policy Press, an imprint of
Bristol University Press
University of Bristol
1-9 Old Park Hill
Bristol
BS2 8BB
UK
t: +44 (0)117 374 6645
e: bup-info@bristol.ac.uk

Details of international sales and distribution partners are available at
policy.bristoluniversitypress.co.uk

British Library Cataloguing in Publication Data
A catalogue record for this book is available from the British Library

ISBN 978-1-4473-6423-8 hardcover
ISBN 978-1-4473-6424-5 paperback
ISBN 978-1-4473-6426-9 ePub
ISBN 978-1-4473-6425-2 ePdf

Cover design: Nicky Borowiec
Front cover image: Irina 27

Bristol University Press and Policy Press use environmentally responsible
print partners.

Printed and bound in Great Britain by CMP, Poole

Contents

List of figures and tables

Figures

Tables

List of abbreviations

AgTech	agriculture technology
AI	artificial intelligence
BD	business development
BLM	Black Lives Matter
B2B	business-to-business
B2U	business-to-university
CBI	Confederation of British Industry
CCF	Connecting Capabilities Fund
CDP	Carbon Disclosure Project
CDT	Centre for Doctoral Training
CEO	chief executive officer
CPD	continuing professional development
CRL	Commercial Readiness Level
CRM	customer relationship management
CSR	corporate social responsibility
CSV	creating shared value
CVC	corporate venture capital
DGM	deep generative model
EAUC	Environmental Association for Universities and Colleges
EDI	equality, diversity and inclusion
ERL	Entrepreneurship Readiness Level
ERVA	Engineering Research Visioning Alliance
ESG	environmental, social and corporate governance
EU	European Union
Exec Ed	executive education
GDP	gross domestic product
GNP	gross national product
GRC	Global Research Council
IIoT	industrial internet of things
IoT	internet of things
IP	intellectual property

IPCC	Intergovernmental Panel on Climate Change
IPR	intellectual property rights
ITF	Impact Taskforce
KE	knowledge exchange
KEC	Knowledge Exchange Concordat
KEF	Knowledge Exchange Framework
KTN	Knowledge Transfer Network
LEP	Local Economic Partnerships
MIT	Massachusetts Institute of Technology
ML	machine learning
MRA	Master Research Agreement
M2M	machine-to-machine
MVP	Minimum Viable Partnership
NCUB	National Centre for Universities and Business
NDA	non-disclosure agreement
NGO	non-governmental organisation
NSF	National Science Foundation
NZIP	Net Zero Innovation Programme
OECD	Organisation for Economic Cooperation and Development
OKR	objectives and key results
OXFo	Oxford Foundry
PoC	Point of Concept
PR	public relations
PRME	Principles for Responsible Management Education
R&D	research and development
R&I	research and innovation
REF	Research Excellence Framework
RFP	Request for Proposal
ROI	return on investment
SLT	senior leadership team
SME	small and medium-sized enterprise
SoW	Statement of Work
SSHA	Social Sciences, Humanities and Arts
STEM	Science, Technology, Engineering and Maths
TEF	Teaching Excellence Framework
TRL	Technology Readiness Level
TTO	Technology Transfer Office

UIDP	University–Industry Demonstration Partnership
UIIN	University Industry Innovation Partnership
UKRI	UK Research and Innovation
UN	United Nations
UN SDGs	UN Sustainable Development Goals
USP	unique selling point
VC	vice chancellor
VP	vice provost
VSEM	Vision, Strategy, Execution, Metrics
WEAll	Wellbeing Economy Alliance
WEF	World Economic Forum
WEGo	Wellbeing Economy Governments
WHO	World Health Organization

About the authors

Tim Bodley-Scott is a Strategic Alliances Director at University College London (UCL) within the Computer Science department, where he develops transformational strategic alliances with key industry and academic partners.

Ersel Oymak is Strategic Alliances Advisor and Innovator in Residence for UCL and Board Member for PraxisAuril. He was formerly Head of Strategic Alliances Directors and Corporate Relationships for UCL and an Advisory Board Member at Hounslow Chamber of Commerce. He has significant global technology sector experience with leading corporates including CISCO, working closely with government, industry and start-ups.

Acknowledgements

Firstly, we would like to thank our extended families, especially our wonderful wives Vicky Scott and Etelka Veronika Oymak and our children, for their support throughout the long days and nights spent writing this book.

Secondly, we are indebted to Philippa Grand, Paul Stevens and all the other staff from Bristol University Press and Policy Press who assisted us with the publication process for their guidance and advice.

We truly appreciate the insights shared by mentors, friends and colleagues, including Jane Osborne-Buglear (Butler), Graca Carvalho and Andy Chew.

Finally, we are grateful to all who have encouraged us throughout our careers, including Stephen Wenham, Bob Temple, Cengiz Tarhan and Mustafa Erdem.

Foreword

Professor Sir Anthony Finkelstein CBE FREng

I think I have participated in every form of university–industry relationships over time. These have ranged from complex transnational collaborative programmes involving multiple large corporate partners to small unfunded and ad-hoc collaborations with start-ups. A few 'marriages of convenience', more than a few genuine and lasting partnerships, some that started as one and finished as the other. I should honestly confess that the relationships have met with mixed success. Some have resulted in significant commercial, social and scientific impact; others have, well, how should I put it politely, 'generated the specified deliverables'. I am not sure that (prior to reading this book, of course) you could have anticipated which was which.

Overall, however, I do feel qualified by virtue of my experience to set out some general lessons. Here, in no particular order, are my top ten personal pointers.

- *Take the time to know each other.* Very few of the collaborative successes have been instant. Most have been preceded by a significant period of mutual familiarisation. Knowing each other's background and trajectory makes a vast difference.
- *Look for complementarity.* Good partnerships are enriched by differing perspectives. Closely aligned expertise may make initial conversations easier but may ultimately lead to a less productive relationships.
- *Honesty is the best policy.* Good partnerships make progress when each party is clear about their priority outcomes. Thus, and for example, industry has commercial imperatives, while universities are assessed by their publication track record. These can be made to complement each other but the drivers need to be understood from the outset.

- *Share values.* While complementary interests can support partnerships, values need to be aligned. These need to be the values that are lived, not simply stated.
- *Agree timelines.* Surprisingly, timelines and differing expectations of what can and should be produced, and when, are a very frequent cause of relationship breakdown. It might be thought, crudely, that industry is more oriented to the short term and universities to the longer term, when in fact the picture is a good deal more complex: product development can be lengthy, while research and funding deadlines are short. Mutual acknowledgement is key.
- *Fairly value your contribution.* Universities tend to overvalue the creativity, expertise and insight that gives rise to an idea and undervalue the patience, capital and commercial nous that an industry partner delivers and which allows that idea to realise its full value. A fair and balanced appreciation of what each party brings to the table is an essential foundation for the success of a partnership.
- *No secrets.* It is surprisingly common for industry partners to keep their commercial and competitive imperatives confidential from their university partners. Similarly, it is common for university partners not to be entirely transparent about their funding arrangements and the tangled relationships between background and foreground work. Bluntly, this is no basis for a partnership.
- *Anticipate commercial tension.* Industrial partners think universities lack agility and want excessive control over intellectual property. Universities think industrial partners impose exploitative terms and conditions and do not want to share the upside. A robust negotiation is OK and can coexist with a strong partnership, as long as each party see an effective commercial arrangement as reinforcing the partnership rather than threatening it.
- *Individuals matter.* However 'strategic' a partnership may be, it is ultimately made to work by individuals who have got to know and trust each other. Nobody can expect a relationship to work if the people concerned move on, or change, with regularity.
- *Align around purpose.* Universities exist in service to a mission. Increasingly, industry recognises the centrality of social purpose.

Shared goals beyond immediate commercial objectives can act as a strong glue for a lasting partnership.

I congratulate Tim and Ersel for their work on this important book. Readers have the opportunity to learn from these experts how to build and sustain transformational partnerships in the service of the UN SDGs. I share their vision and am encouraged that, following the insights and guidance, we can create a new generation of partnerships that stretch beyond the transactional relationships of the past.

Preface

This book is aimed at a variety of people from different backgrounds including practitioners and brokers of university–industry partnerships (Figure 0.1). This may include:

- knowledge exchange (KE), business development (BD) and industry-facing academics who wish to be more effective at interacting with industry, in diverse geographies (this could include both those inside tech transfer offices and those based in departments);
- leaders 'at all levels' with a focus on research, external engagement, innovation and entrepreneurship, corporate relations and fundraising;
- university relations leads within corporates and their philanthropic foundations;
- other philanthropic foundations;
- academics and Master of Business Administration (MBA) students with interests including innovation management, university–industry relations (the interface between academic science and industry), organisation theory, entrepreneurship and regional economic development;
- government policy advisors interested in maximising economic and societal benefits from innovative university–industry–government–civil society–environment 'quintuple helix' relationships within a knowledge economy.[1] These relationships are even more vital as we face the global grand challenges, including the climate emergency. This audience would also include funding agency staff from UK Research and Innovation (UKRI), Knowledge Transfer Network (KTN) and Catapults;
- non-governmental organisations (NGOs), including the United Nations (UN), Organisation for Economic Co-operation and Development (OECD), World Bank and

professional associations and societies, interested in research and innovation for public benefit. Internationally professional associations of knowledge exchange practitioners such as the University–Industry Demonstration Partnership (UIDP) and University Industry Innovation Network (UIIN) are also a very relevant audience;

- venture capital and sovereign wealth funds interested in 'impact investing' who wish to learn how to best engage with universities to discover transformational technological solutions to challenging global problems such as the UN Sustainable Development Goals (UN SDGs).

Figure 0.1: The different audiences that we have written this book for

Why now?

More than ever before, practitioners of university–industry relationships require tools to identify, govern and share joint value leveraged through bringing together complementary assets and capabilities. In our experience and interactions with senior industry figures, we have seen the necessity and huge potential to align strategy explicitly with achieving grand challenges such as the UN SDGs to achieve global societal benefit. The SDGs are not a perfect blueprint of an ideal world, but they are a great start. The only way to make progress against the scale and complexity of current globally concerning issues is through strong, multifaceted partnerships that draw on a wide range of expertise, diverse and innovative thinking and socially just solutions.

We aim to inspire, motivate and equip practitioners from multiple sectors to see the value of transformational alliances to solve global challenges and form greater cross-border collaborations between the Global North and South that will bring positive change. Our passion is to help industry and academia particularly to work together more effectively for wider societal benefit, by creating mutual value for universities and industry.

This is not an empirical study of university–industry partnerships, rather a practitioner account based on our experience, insights and conversations with innovative university and corporate leaders from around the world in different research and development (R&D) contexts and based around real-life case studies to evidence our principles. These case studies have been anonymised for the purposes of this book.

Through reflection on professional practice, we have developed the theory of the 5th generation university, for example. Throughout the book, we adopt a layered approach, examining partnerships at different scales – local, regional, national, international – and provide relevant management insights for departmental, faculty and central university business units.

This book identifies and shares best practices gained from years of experience working with corporates, small and medium-sized enterprises (SMEs), and start-ups. We have seen that our transformational approach to developing, managing and leading alliances may be applied to engaging all sizes of companies. In our experience, smaller companies can be more accessible as their senior leaders are easier to approach and collaborate with in a timely manner.[2] However, the industry partner we focus on for this book is typically a large, global corporate with the scale to make a significant impact on achieving the UN SDGs.

A holistic approach to collaboration will enable universities to organise their activities to deliver outstanding public benefit and maximise opportunities to make positive impact at scale on their regions as well as nationally and internationally. This book offers a comprehensive holistic framework covering both programmatic activities and philanthropic considerations that will create a step-change in how you approach partnership and collaboration. The authors have a combined 45 years of experience working at the interface between universities, business and government.

1

A journey from transactional to transformational alliances

'If working apart, we are a force powerful enough to destabilise our planet. Surely working together, we are powerful enough to save it. In my lifetime, I've witnessed a terrible decline. In your lifetimes, you could and should witness a wonderful recovery. That desperate hope ladies and gentlemen, delegates, excellencies, is why the world is looking to you and why you are here. Thank you.'

Sir David Attenborough's speech
at COP26 summit, October 2021

Our journey

Several years ago, a major bank ran an advert about a Museum of Procrastination in which a visitor was welcomed by a steward to an exhibition on the topic of 'where we put our good intentions that never fully materialised'. The visitor was then taken on a guided tour through different sections of the museum. This included the gym section, where memberships were used only once and then spent the rest of their lives in wallets, untouched. The tour then went on through the 'unfinished novels section', where novels that could have been inspirational works of art were on display. Next, the visitor was escorted into a gallery space where there were hundreds of unused musical instruments. Finally, the last room on the tour, and arguably the saddest, showcased the millions of ideas, inventions and eureka moments that people had abandoned before they could have been of any use to society. The tour guide's conclusion was that 'some of these could actually revolutionise the way we live our lives'.

Universities must never become Museums of Procrastination like the advert depicted, where diverse talent, creativity, inspiration, and problem-solving is wasted. The advert's tagline messaging is 'There is always the temptation to put off until tomorrow, what you could do today. There is no time like the present to follow your ambitions, no matter how big or small, and we are here to support you in any way we can'.[1]

We have worked with leading universities, business and government for many years, and believe that now, more than ever, universities must help students on their way to achieving their ambitions – not just to secure a good job, but also to bring about positive change in the world, for the good of humanity. Universities must become more focused on being the best 'for' the world, rather than just the best 'in' the world according to certain rankings based mainly around research quality. We have seen first-hand that the best way for universities to do this and rediscover their role as a public good is through partnership for positive change.

Universities exist to attract, inspire, nurture and harness extraordinary talent for the good of society – and not just to have good intentions that do not fully materialise. Forward-thinking universities, or 'Next Generation Universities', are ambitious about demonstrating great societal value (both social and economic impact) to achieve the 'common good'. To realise this, at pace and scale, they will partner with like-minded organisations, whether in academia, industry or civil society. They have no boundaries in imagining how the world can be improved through effective collaboration.

Uluru in the centre of Australia is the largest known monolith or single massive stone or rock in the world. It is 2.2 miles long and extends several miles deep underground, although no one is sure exactly how far. Through our work in the corporate engagement and philanthropy team for a major campus expansion project, we realised that universities are like giant monoliths, with many powerful features that remain largely hidden underground, difficult for potential partners to discover. This must change if the world is to tackle climate change and other pressing

2

societal challenges, since no single organisation can solve such problems alone.

Universities can achieve so much more through partnership. Humans have so far explored only 1 per cent of the world's ocean depths. University–industry collaborations through research, teaching and knowledge exchange (KE) have probably achieved only 1 per cent of what is possible to be discovered together through partnership.

Like many people, 2020 brought a year of adversity and employment challenges for us personally. While we were adjusting to the 'new different' of being on furlough leave from our roles, we had space to reflect on what really mattered in our lives. For us, this meant our families, friends and how we can build a better world for our children post-pandemic. We started to write this book setting out a new, more ambitious co-innovation approach to KE and corporate engagement that would tackle pressing global challenges beyond COVID-19 and achieve broad societal benefit. We wanted to set out the lessons and insights we had learned from our own diverse experiences that we felt could help our own and future generations to achieve positive change through collaboration.

We have extensive experience managing public, private and voluntary sector partnerships, improving income generation, and growing KE, research and teaching activity with impact. Multifaceted, coordinated collaboration and partnership activity has a critical role in KE. Our highly collaborative approach has been validated by a myriad of executives from leading global firms who have highlighted the importance of the UN Sustainable Development Goals (SDGs) for their future business models and investment decisions.

Both incremental and disruptive collaborative innovation (co-innovation) for the common good can have a tremendous impact on achieving the UN SDGs. When the UN SDGs were developed, the importance of partnership for achieving the goals was recognised by one of the goals itself being 'partnership' (SDG 17). This book aims to contribute to achieving all the SDGs by focusing on this vital underpinning goal.

We offer this book as a guide to help higher education make the turn towards becoming fit for the next generation, where institutions of research, education and innovation prioritise transformational change for the good of humanity by effectively addressing the UN SDGs. We highlight new insights about the future of alliances and explain how both universities and corporates can work together more effectively for mutual and societal benefit.

The role of university–industry collaboration to achieve the UN Sustainable Development Goals

In the post-pandemic era, there are a couple of key questions that need answering effectively:

- How can universities help countries to build stronger, mutually beneficial and holistic partnerships with industry for the common good?
- How should the organisational structures and the focus of university-business collaboration adopt new ways to accommodate the 'new normal'?

In the US, industry funding to academia for research and development (R&D) was worth approximately $10 billion in 2020.[2] If current trends continue, China will overtake the US by 2025 to fund more R&D than any other country. It already funds more R&D than the four next-highest countries (Japan, Germany, South Korea and France) combined.

While we see KE as being far more than just commercialisation of R&D, technology transfer is relatively easy to measure and, according to a study funded by the Biotechnology Industry Organisation and the Association of University Technology Managers, the impact of university technology transfer in the US alone from 1996 to 2007 was a $457 billion addition to gross industrial output, a $187 billion positive impact on US gross national product (GNP) and at least 279,000 new jobs across the US created due to university-licensed products commercialised by industry.[3]

A successful alliance between academia and industry requires all the components in the complex structures of universities and the corporates to create new dynamics and act together in harmony with sufficient resources in place.

Universities have many important assets that are attractive to industry partners (see Figure 1.1):

- people – leading multidisciplinary academic and professional services experts with specialist knowledge who may have a track record of working with industry, combined with independence and credibility;
- location – a university is often an 'anchor institution' within a locality, and proximity to industry can be a significant pull factor for certain companies looking to form partnerships that will leverage talent from the surrounding region;
- brand – particularly their reputation as being recognised for the quality of their research, teaching, innovation, and graduates and the opportunities this presents for brand association and corporate philanthropy;
- technology – creating new processes and solutions to problems through access to advanced labs, equipment and facilities;
- talent – innovative, highly skilled and diverse student population;
- influence – the opportunity to align with government around key industrial, research and innovation strategies, to target priorities for broader societal benefit and the ability to bring diverse cross-sector stakeholders together in a neutral space.

Figure 1.1: University assets: what universities can offer to align with and complement industry resources

Alliances, partnerships, acquisitions, mergers and joint ventures are now common denominators in most businesses as part of their core strategy for achieving higher targets and goals. Corporates increasingly look to external partnerships for acquiring even more strategic resources and capabilities. They need a practical roadmap to ensure these relationships generate value, and so corporates consider questions like:

- What combinations of complementary resources are needed to make this partnership a success?
- How should these resources be managed over time?
- Will the outputs of these partnerships offer a return on investment?

In his book *Remix Strategy: The Three Laws of Business Combinations* (2015),[4] author Benjamin Gomes-Casseres suggests a clear path to effectively answering these questions with the following headlines:

- 'Enable joint value creation'
- 'Ensure effective governance to realise value'
- 'Ensure value sharing and a return on investment or reward for both parties'

Leading corporates have the following main objectives in working with academia (see further Table 1.2):

- access and build a talent pipeline through participating in innovative student projects, offering summer internships, graduate employment and funding postgraduate scholarships, fellowships and chairs;
- research, develop and commercialise the best-of-breed technology through co-innovation;
- strengthen brand through thought leadership in partnership with academic experts, and projects focused on achieving societal benefit;
- leverage government funding and influence.

In September 2015, 193 countries officially adopted the 17 UN SDGs at a historic UN summit. World leaders agreed to mobilise efforts to 'end all forms of poverty, fight inequalities and tackle climate change, while ensuring that no one is left behind'.[5] The SDGs, also known as Global Goals, followed on from the success of the Millennium Development Goals (MDGs), aiming to go further to end poverty in its many forms. The SDGs support sustainable economic growth to promote prosperity and address societal needs while protecting the planet. Although they are not legally binding, the SDGs universally apply to all, and task governments to deliver on behalf of both people and planet.

The SDGs offer a way for countries and their universities and companies to work together across the globe to find solutions for the benefit of humanity. They can have a similar effect to that of international trade as a driver of peaceful, productive relations between states around common interests.

Governments should consider how their relationships with academia, industry and civil society (the quadruple helix) can be strengthened, not just for their national self-interest, but now for global benefit. How can the industrial strategies of governments contribute to broader transitions such as the move to a zero-carbon economy that makes a significant impact towards mitigating climate change and achieving several UN SDGs?

A report called 'How to design a successful industrial strategy' (2020), written by the Institute for Government think-tank, recommends governments choose objectives that 'go with the grain of other non-economic goals'.[6] Alongside the shift to a zero-carbon economy, they also highlight ageing and the future of mobility as two other trends. Within the quadruple helix collaboration model (Figure 1.2), each type of organisation or 'actor' is vital for success. The quadruple helix concept has been applied to European Union (EU)-sponsored projects and policies. This includes the EU–MACS (European Market for Climate Services) project,[7] and the European Commission's Open Innovation 2.0 (OI2) policy for a digital single market that supports open innovation and regional innovation systems.[8]

Expanding on this concept we find the analogy of the Olympic Games to be useful. Just as the Olympic symbol has five rings representing a union of five continents taking part in the Games, the quintuple helix visualises the collective interaction and

Figure 1.2: The multi-sector roles within quadruple and quintuple helix partnerships to achieve societal benefit

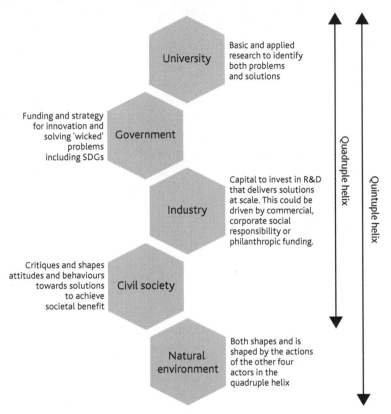

exchange of knowledge in a knowledge economy by means of five helices, each with complementary assets:

- education system – intellectual and human capital or 'assets' dominate;
- political system – legislative assets dominate;
- economic system – financial assets dominate;
- media-based public – cultural assets dominate;
- natural environment – natural assets dominate.

International cooperation agreements such as COP26, focused on reducing climate change by maintaining a 1.5° temperature rise by 2100, will be dependent on strong, transformational quintuple helix alliances that incorporate the impact of quadruple actors on the environment (Figure 1.2).

Defining alliances

Why should universities orientate transformational strategic alliances around the UN SDGs? The basic reason is that they provide an extremely practical and important framework to demonstrate the impact of their research, teaching and innovation to achieve social good.

As the ecological environment is a key focus area for the SDGs, the model in Figure 1.3 becomes a quintuple helix where issues such as biodiversity loss and excessive resource extraction from the natural world are seen as vital challenges that need to be tackled through transformational partnership.

The range of different partnerships and alliances typically includes a wide spectrum of increasingly complex relationships.

Figure 1.3: Quintuple helix partnerships are channelled towards UN Global Goals with an ecological focus, through a multi-sector challenge-driven, mission-focused approach[9]

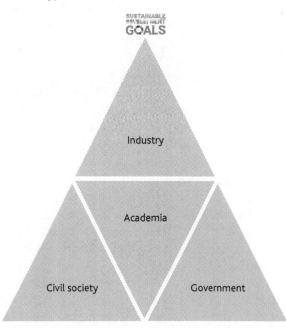

At the lowest collaboration and complexity level are transactional relationships involving a one-way, purchase-based engagement with minimal co-value creation. At the other end of the spectrum are transformational, multi-sector alliances that have the highest level of impact, trust, and co-value creation opportunity. These include university–industry and multi-sector alliances that bring together academia, government, civil society and industry.

Transformational alliances involve very high levels of joint planning of activity, for example to rapidly scale efforts towards addressing urgent global challenges such as the climate emergency. These multi-sector alliances are often large-scale collaborations that are multifaceted and multidimensional in nature. They involve research, teaching and KE and require a highly aligned shared vision, strong leadership and trust. In between the two extremes are more standard strategic alliances that are typical within many leading universities and corporates today.

Alliances, like partnerships, can mean different things to different people; however, we see alliances as typically deeper relationships than partnerships. In Figure 1.4, we describe strategic and transformational alliances as requiring more trust and delivering more co-value creation and impact than transactional relationships and tactical partnerships. This is because strategic alliances are generally longer in duration and more complex, involving greater joint business planning and trust. Alliances therefore enable organisations to achieve more together than they can do alone. As the English poet John Donne famously said: 'no man is an island', highlighting the interdependence of humanity.[10] Likewise, in today's world of interlocking, transdisciplinary challenges, no forward-thinking university or company can afford to exist as an institutional island without any meaningful external engagement.

We use the term 'strategic alliances' to mean highly collaborative and aligned deep business-to-business (B2B) relationships where there is an agreement to work together for mutual benefit. We refer to 'transformational strategic alliances' to expand on the conventional understanding of strategic alliances. We consider the purpose of 'transformation' of both parties' organisations and wider society as the most important reason to forge an alliance. In the future it is likely that there will be a growth in ecosystems

Figure 1.4: The spectrum of collaborative relationships between universities and industry

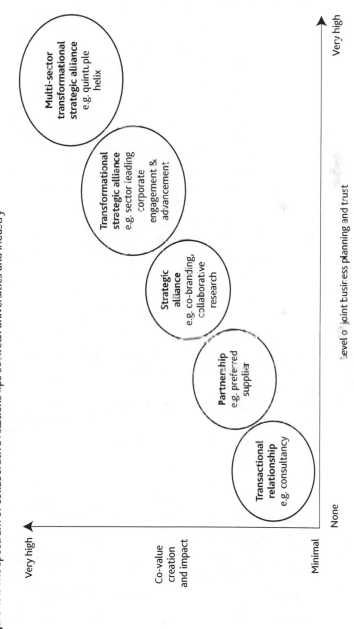

of transformational multi-partner and multi-sector alliances to address societal challenges that no single organisation is able to solve alone.

Gravitational waves occur when two black holes collide and send out enormously powerful waves that squash, stretch and transform space and time. When the two sectors of academia and industry collide through alliances, we argue that the result can also be transformational, both internally within the respective organisations as well as externally for society. Transformational strategic alliances are about creating long-term joint value and impact through a deep, mutually beneficial, and special category of B2B partnership. All successful alliances involve ever-deepening relationships between multiple key staff and brokers in both organisations.

A university and a corporate can legitimately claim to have a transformational strategic alliance related to achieving the UN SDGs when the following foundational Five Pillars are in place (as shown in Table 1.1).

Table 1.1: The Five Pillars of transformational strategic alliances

Pillars	Description
1	Shared vision, mission and values, including a sense of ethical obligation and compassion towards the world's poorest and most vulnerable people, combined with a sense of humility.
2	A focus on measuring success against achieving positive change for the benefit of global humanity.
3	A bold, courageous, creative, inspirational and servant leadership approach to engagement, both internally and externally, from the top down that is open to multifaceted research, teaching, knowledge exchange, innovation, and collaboration through deep, impactful alliances.
4	An openness to being part of wider, even globalised, innovation ecosystems within mission-focused triple, quadruple, or quintuple helix networks to scale and achieve greater 'transformational collaborative advantage'. This concept refers to new models of working together rather than in competition to achieve social innovation and wide societal benefit, impacting whole industry sectors.
5	A highly aligned, agile, strategic, and operational management approach that recognises, rewards and values the contribution of all partners. Through this, each party can release and realise value through effective, adaptable execution at scale.

Transformational alliances are one of the key interventions that universities can make to support a new paradigm of mission-focused activity addressing the UN SDGs (set out in Figure 1.5).

Figure 1.5: The 17 United Nations Sustainable Development Goals (UN SDGs)[11]

Source: www.un.org

A notable recent trend is that corporates are reducing the overall number of universities that they collaborate with but are looking to form deeper relationships with a limited number of academic institutions. These alliances often have multiple forms of interactions between universities and industry covering the following:

- R&D collaboration;
- entrepreneurial activity, for example involvement in supporting student and staff spinouts;
- academic and student mobility, for example internships;
- continuing professional development (CPD), executive education (Exec Ed), lifelong learning and workforce development;
- community outreach activity, for example to schools;
- curriculum co-design and delivery;
- co-innovation;

- commercialisation/technology transfer through creation of intellectual property rights (IPR);
- advancement through corporate philanthropy.

Business-to-university (B2U) relationships are a special type of B2B interaction since universities are themselves businesses but ones with different objectives and constraints. B2U relationships are set to replace B2B as offering the greatest co-value creation if managed effectively. Indeed, they have the potential to be far more strategic since universities are generally rarely in competition with industry. They have far more to gain through transformational collaborative advantage as stated in Pillar 4 (see Table 1.1). This value comes from the potential for such alliances to transform whole industry sectors through transdisciplinary, mission-focused, challenge-led innovation.

Knowledge exchange: more than a 'third mission'

KE encompasses a rich tapestry of different pathways for knowledge to be diffused bi-directionally from universities into industry and vice versa. In the UK's Knowledge Exchange Concordat (KEC), this is defined as:

> a collaborative, creative endeavour that translates knowledge and research into impact in society and the economy. KE includes a set of activities, processes and skills that enable close collaboration between universities and partner organisations to deliver commercial, environmental, cultural and place-based benefits, opportunities for students and increased prosperity.[12]

It includes the commercialisation of academic knowledge through innovation and enterprise, although this must not be seen as the sole focus. Indeed, we argue that the right vision of KE and impact is far broader than just commercialisation. KE has often been seen as a 'third mission' for universities alongside their core research and teaching roles. However, a combination of factors has led to leading universities now seeing KE as underpinning, and on equal terms with, research and education.

The perception and relative importance of KE varies around the world. In many regions it is still seen as mainly about technology transfer and commercialisation. In the UK, however, KE is largely recognised as being far broader than just technology transfer or spinout creation and licensing. It is, at the very least, about bidirectional, mutual learning through collaboration, rather than a linear, unidirectional flow or 'pipeline' from universities to industry. We prefer the term 'exchange' to 'transfer' (often used in North America), as it encompasses this understanding of a two-way, mutually beneficial conversation between universities and industry, to build something together (co-creation) of genuine value to society. Such co-creation also listens to voices from civil society and local government to unleash real value and transformation to their regions. They do this by reflecting together on how the UN SDGs can be realised locally. Globally, there is huge potential to see positive change when a more holistic definition of KE is widely accepted and cross-sector transformational alliances become the norm for addressing the UN SDGs.

Extract 44 from the 2016 National Centre for Universities and Business (NCUB) Report illustrates the many diverse forms of KE between universities and external organisations including industry partners. Academics from across the subject disciplines engage with KE activities.[13] Forward-thinking universities recognise that approaching problem solving through cross-disciplinary engagement is very attractive to external partners from industry, government, philanthropic foundations and non-governmental organisations (NGOs) to help to grow transformational strategic alliances. Innovative academic institutions have formed transformational alliances based on their strengths and capabilities in specific fields such as water management within Dutch universities. In this example, these capabilities are often linked to the challenges of geographical context such as the low-lying landscape prone to flooding within the Netherlands.

How can universities apply their knowledge for wider benefit across the world? A brief answer to this is by cultivating alliances through adoption of an innovative approach to knowledge sharing with application to the developing world, also known as the Global South, to achieve the UN SDGs by collaboration.

Alliance goals for universities and industry – why collaborate?

Universities and industry need to collaborate to survive and thrive in the knowledge economy of the 21st century. The many complex societal challenges facing the world mean that no single organisation, however large, has all the necessary skills and capabilities to find solutions independently. Even the most innovative companies recognise that they do not have the monopoly on talent to tackle the biggest technological and scientific problems, for example addressing climate change. Instead, they see the benefit in sourcing a diversity of talent from outside their organisations, particularly from approachable universities, to accelerate their research and innovation.

Strategic alliances are nothing new. Tribes and nations throughout history have formed alliances for mutual interest, for example for security and protection. Today, such alliances include the USA, the EU and, more recently, the African Union. Since the birth of corporations, in the last 200 years general business goals have led to B2B alliances between corporations for the following reasons:

- to fix a short-term problem in a current product line;
- to develop long-term R&D that could lead to future product lines – 'emerging innovation';
- to gain exposure to new start-ups that companies may wish to acquire;
- to enhance their joint marketing and public relations (PR);
- to achieve market access and political influence in uncharted territories.

For industry engagement with universities, there are several more key B2U drivers that need to be considered in the strategic thinking of corporates (see Table 1.2):

Priorities for universities, on the other hand, include:

- access to real-world problems and case studies for teaching, research and demonstrating impact. This is increasingly important to public funding bodies;

Table 1.2: Business-to-university drivers for university–industry collaboration

B2U drivers	Description
1	To build their talent pipeline in a particular region or with a university that has a strong reputation in one or more relevant subject areas as well as to retain talent through workforce development, such as offering bespoke short courses or PhD opportunities for technical staff
2	To mitigate operational risk in developing technology services and solutions by gaining expert, independent insights on the latest research directions, the underpinning science, and important ethical considerations
3	To explore datasets and find new insights from multidisciplinary experts using a diversity of novel techniques
4	To participate with groups of universities in pre-competitive, open-source consortia interested in shaping the direction of regulation or standards and addressing challenges facing across industry sectors
5	To gain political influence through leveraging state funding opportunities
6	To explore new domain areas through student projects and demonstrators that could become new markets as well as engagement with the university start-up ecosystem

- access to industry resources (financial, data, expertise and so on);
- access to strategic corporate philanthropy and industry income as public funding for university-based R&D reduces, in some Western countries particularly.

'Blue Ocean Strategy': pioneering market creating innovation through collaboration

The linear model of university–industry interactions shown in Figure 1.6 involves building partnerships and alliances from initial short-term transactional projects. This process is linear in terms of the evolution of organisational learning and institutional innovation about how to build strong partnerships at every management level. This requires organisations to gain the necessary capability and skills to work effectively and cooperatively across the different layers and teams within the university.

Figure 1.6: Comparing different forms of university–industry relationships

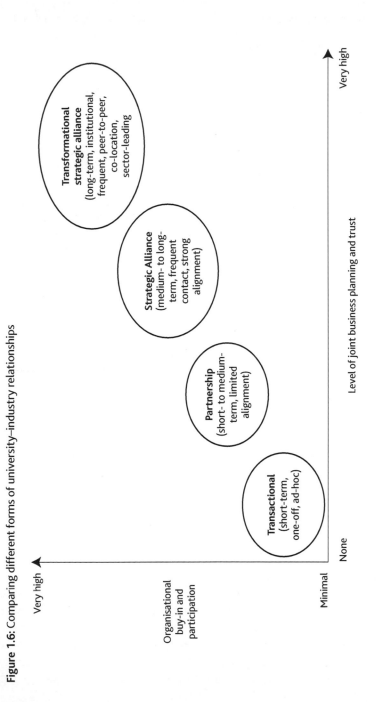

As interactions become more frequent and complex, a well-managed alliance acts as a point of coordination and a catalyst for progress. This is where strategic alliance functionality within a university or industry, regardless of R&D context, becomes a source of 'collaborative advantage', helping these organisations to proactively shape their environments in an era of rapid socioeconomic change and to move beyond merely competing. For instance, the pharmaceutical sector is generally advanced at forming strategic alliances with universities due to the long-term requirements to accommodate the time needed for clinical trials. However, many companies in other sectors do not have the same depth of experience and tacit knowledge gained through extensive university collaboration.

The concept of 'Blue Ocean Strategy' developed in 2005 by Professors W. Chan Kim and Renée Mauborgne suggests that forward-thinking organisations can move from seeing themselves surrounded in a 'Red Ocean' environment of highly competitive sharks to become 'Blue Oceans' with little or no competition.[14] Is this possible or too idealistic? The marketisation of higher education, particularly in the West, has led to many universities becoming increasingly competitive in a sector that has historically been very low in competition. They have become weighed down by bureaucracy unable to escape their Red Oceans of competitive thinking, obsessed with rebranding exercises and capturing new 'customers'. There would be great benefits for universities and industry to focus more on 'creating a larger economic pie for all' rather than just competing intensively within their own market spaces.

In 2017, the same authors provided examples of Blue Ocean strategy in action within many different organisations, including non-profits and governments, explaining what a 'Blue Ocean Shift' in mindset looked like: 'expanding mental horizons and shifting understanding of where opportunity lies'.[15] Essentially, this was about moving from market-competing to market-creating innovation. Such a way of thinking opens new possibilities for universities and industry, often enabling higher value at lower cost through collaboration. However, we recognise that there will always be competition in the market, although a transition towards co-opetition is likely to win out. This is where competition and collaboration coexist in a balanced way to create mutual new opportunities and positive change.

So how can universities become pioneers of market-creating innovation? Transformational strategic alliance teams have the opportunity-based, entrepreneurial thinking necessary to form new multi-sector quadruple and quintuple helix aware partnerships that create shared value for the university by thinking about the globally excluded. For example, this includes those people who are unable to access clean drinking water or adequate nutrition in Sub-Saharan Africa.

How can universities avoid fragmentation in external engagement?

Often external engagement within universities is very fragmented with no overarching strategy, no or few clear lines of communication and little governance. For example, all the following central university teams in Figure 1.7 are likely to have significant external engagements with industry, government and civil society as well as with individual academics in departments.

University leaders should have a designated executive champion for external engagement and should consider the scope for integrating external engagement functions to ensure improved internal communication and operational delivery of alliance activity. Leading universities are already changing their structures to ensure a greater focus on alliances. At the University of Cambridge, they now have a Strategic Partnerships Office (SPO) that:

> works with the Schools, Faculties and Departments to create, identify, and disseminate opportunities for strategic collaboration across all disciplines and countries; and to negotiate, structure and implement strategic partnership agreements. The SPO is made up of the Public Institutional Partnerships Team, which manages formal collaborations between Cambridge and other universities and research institutions, and the Business Partnerships Team, which manages formal relationships between Cambridge and industry partners.[16]

Figure 1.7: The university functions that have a strong external engagement focus

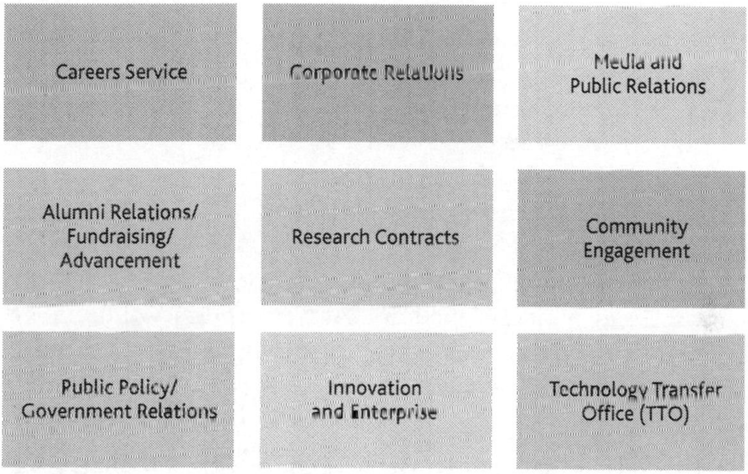

Careers Service	Corporate Relations	Media and Public Relations
Alumni Relations/ Fundraising/ Advancement	Research Contracts	Community Engagement
Public Policy/ Government Relations	Innovation and Enterprise	Technology Transfer Office (TTO)

Different knowledge exchange structures in universities and industry

University KE activities are structured and managed in a wide range of different ways that could include staff working in central teams as well as within academic departments and faculties. Potential industry partners may not be aware that each university has a different governance structure through which lines of accountability and decision making around external engagement will flow. This could be through a matrix-based approach in which both academic and professional services staff have authority for signing off corporate framework agreements.

In the US and the UK, responsibility for KE activities generally comes under the remit of a Vice Provost (Research) or Vice President (Research). Individual KE-focused units within a university may include:

- research support;
- industry liaison/corporate engagement;
- technology transfer office (TTO) or company;
- commercialisation institute;
- innovation hubs, incubators, accelerators and post-accelerators.

Key business functions within industry involved in university partnerships may include:

- business units or operations with a focus on short-term business goals;
- R&D (mainly a function within advanced and emerging technology business units with a longer-term focus);
- human resources/talent management;
- marketing and business development.

It is important for alliance professionals to engage with the most relevant business functions within corporates and, where necessary to communicate across functions, to ensure effective coordination of KE activity.

New trends: Impact investment, Tech for Good, Industry 4.0 and university accelerators

According to reports released in 2017 by the Business and Sustainable Development Commission,[17] and the World Economic Forum and Accenture Analysis,[18] technology for solving the UN SDGs presents a $12 trillion global opportunity up to 2030, when the UN SDGs are to be achieved. Many of these technologies will be related to a move towards a net zero-carbon economy to achieve SDG 13 'Climate Action' as society seeks to build back (or forward) better.

There has been a global growth in socially motivated capital among pension funds and venture capitalists. This is also known as the 'impact investment' movement and aims to combine purpose and profit and to achieve a 'triple bottom line': generating sustainable value for business and society. According to the Global Steering Group for Impact Investment, impact investments are 'investments made with an explicit intention to generate positive, measurable social and environmental impact alongside a financial return. Impact investment optimises risk, return and impact to benefit people and the planet.'[19]

Impact-driven business has a significant role to play in building a greener, safer, inclusive and connected future. New investment funds in this area are emerging and more traditional funds are adapting investment criteria to align with the UN SDGs and address global challenges. London is currently Europe's #1 for 'Tech for Good' or 'social tech'. Tech companies under this banner have identified pressing social challenges, often linked to the UN SDGs, and are applying technology to deliver solutions.

The Tech for Good movement offers a great opportunity for universities to grow their entrepreneurial ecosystem and harness funding from investors for social good. Alliances with corporates offering mentoring and training offer a way for Tech for Good start-ups to scale faster than they could do otherwise.

Is this a compassionate turn for global capitalism that will lead to a more inclusive and sustainable global economy? Let's hope so. It certainly offers great opportunities for universities to leverage funding and investment for research, development and innovation towards addressing the UN SDGs. The world needs transformative change, which means that governments, charities, venture capitalists, philanthropists and academia must work together and find new ways to partner for social good in a way that contributes to society.

Investment leaders do not see impact as just another venture capital (VC) category focused on social innovation. It is about the creation of an ecosystem of transdisciplinary alliances to seek solutions for fair and just recoveries from the COVID-19 crisis. Sarah Gordon, chief executive officer (CEO) of the Impact Investing Institute, said:

> Impact investment has the potential to contribute to solutions to some of the biggest challenges we face – whether that is a just recovery from the pandemic or addressing the climate crisis. To harness private capital at scale for public good, we need structures that meet investors' requirements and deploy capital where it is needed, improving access to decent jobs, education, and healthcare, and investing in a just transition to a net-zero world.[20]

As part of the UK's G7 2021 presidency, an independent Impact Taskforce (ITF) was created to come up with solutions for a sustainable and inclusive recovery from the pandemic and promote impact-driven economies and societies in the long term. The ITF will:

- foster and facilitate discussions and recommendations around impact transparency, integrity and trust;
- investigate ways to create financial vehicles that can deliver investments for the benefit of people and planet worldwide. It will 'actively look to advance impact investment in low and middle-income countries hit hard by the pandemic.'[21]

Commenting on the formation of the ITF, Nick Hurd, a former UK Member of Parliament and Minister, who chairs the Access Foundation for Social Investment and led the UK government's work to scale the development of the impact investment market between 2010 and 2015, is the chair of the Impact Taskforce. He said:

> The state of our world requires a change in mindset from governments and the market. It will not be enough for private capital to do less harm. We need to mobilise trillions of dollars into investments that combine return with positive social or environmental impact. The Impact Taskforce will show how that can be done.[22]

The whole approach to investment in tech start-ups is changing. University spinouts and student start-ups in areas such as machine learning, quantum, automation and computer vision will have to demonstrate their positive societal benefit and contribution to the biggest challenges facing the world. They will need sustainable business models to attract investment.

Industry 4.0 firms and next generation universities will need to become more adaptable, agile, customer-centric, and digitally enabled. Impact investors will look for entrepreneurial university teams they can trust with the ideas and capability to scale. The Fourth Industrial Revolution (or Industry 4.0) is the ongoing automation of traditional manufacturing and industrial practices, using modern smart technology. Large-scale machine-to-machine communication (M2M) and the Internet of Things (IoT) are integrated for increased automation, improved communication and self-monitoring, and production of smart machines that can analyse and diagnose issues without the need for human intervention.

Continuing to drive operational efficiencies through traditional cost-cutting measures now provides only marginal gains to industry. Meanwhile, Industry 4.0 is about the significant digital transformation taking place in the way goods are produced and delivered – moving towards industrial automation and the flexible factory. To stay competitive, factories and warehouses must leverage the Industrial Internet of Things (IIoT) and digitalisation to become much more agile and efficient.

While industries have automated many processes, there are still huge opportunities in adjusting to a future zero-carbon, circular economy where universities have the right talent and technology solutions to the most pressing issues of industry to make automation possible on a much larger scale. To generate a greater impact, academia will need, alongside nurturing a strong intellect, the ability to articulate complex ideas persuasively and relevantly to senior industry executives.

Corporates as well as small and medium-sized enterprises (SMEs) must unearth the hidden treasure of working with universities and vice versa. A peer-to-peer transformational strategic alliance can help to develop the most cutting-edge products and solutions that will deliver business benefits alongside positive change for society. Such business outcomes and benefits will be sector leading and sector defining because of this transformational collaborative advantage.

More responsible entrepreneurship driven by universities in alliance with leading corporates and VC could have a huge impact on the UN SDGs. Indeed, in recent years many corporates have founded corporate venture capital (CVC) arms to their business, often with a focus on grand challenge areas such as zero-carbon technologies. Large research-intensive universities increasingly also have investment funds that can be leveraged for social good. Next generation universities consider how they can build capacity for entrepreneurs in the Global South, particularly, where there are often fewer resources for such activity. This may lead to Global North universities opening their investment funds to Global South universities.

Figure 1.8 shows the major stakeholders of the social tech ecosystem. The quintuple helix of government, corporates (through CVC and philanthropy), academia and civil society (service providers within charities, hospitals, schools and the voluntary sector) channelled towards people and planet (environment) are all impacted through the growing social tech movement.

University incubators and accelerators are well placed to engage with this movement through a combination of both commercial 'for profit' and social enterprises created by staff and students to develop 'purpose-driven' tech. For example, Oxford Foundry (OxFo), an accelerator set up by Oxford University's Saïd Business School has 3,300 members developing spinouts and raising funds.[23] OxFo offers free workshops in coding, blockchain, and AI, recognising the increasing importance of upskilling students in digital skills alongside their degree. Setting up accelerators can help universities to build entrepreneurship support and training capacity for both their staff and students as well as gain experience and capability engaging with corporates, venture capital organisations and foundations around start-ups and spinouts.

Social enterprises or ventures are businesses that use their generated surpluses to achieve social objectives, such as reinvesting profits into the sustainability of the business or donating them for

Figure 1.8: The main stakeholders within the social tech ecosystem

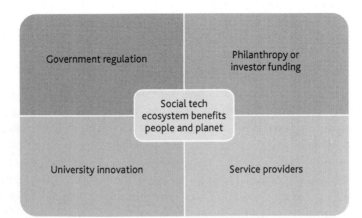

community benefit. The British Council, a big promoter of the benefits of social enterprise and the impact economy, see social enterprise as an important way to address the world's biggest challenges, including the UN SDGs, and bring about positive social change. They offer free online training courses focused on social enterprise via Futurelearn.[24]

In 2018, Rice Inc, a student-led AgTech social enterprise aiming to reduce food poverty in the Global South won the $1m Hult Prize, having beaten 200,000 other ideas.[25] The challenge was to build a sustainable, scalable social enterprise to harness the power of energy to transform the lives of 10 million people. The winning idea achieves this through disrupting the traditional rice supply chain in the region, buying rice directly from farmers and drying it using renewable energy, improving efficiency, and avoiding the 30 per cent spoilage rate. The students behind Rice Inc are also addressing several UN SDGs (see Figure 1.5) through this innovative social entrepreneurship:

- SDG 1 – No poverty
- SDG 2 – Zero hunger
- SDG 3 – Good health and well-being
- SDG 7 – Affordable and clean energy
- SDG 9 – Industry, innovation and infrastructure
- SDG 12 – Responsible consumption and production
- SDG 15 – Life on land
- SDG 17 – Partnerships for the goals

The Hult Prize[26] is the world's largest platform and accelerator for the creation and launch of sustainable, impact-focused start-ups emerging from universities worldwide, and on the judging panel are industry CEOs from some of the world's leading manufacturing and telecommunications corporations.

Sectors with historical low investment in R&D and with below-average productivity, such as agriculture, are ripe for innovation that can bring both business benefit and address the UN SDGs. One example is a promising digital platform founded in 2015 used by small-scale farmers in the Global South to crowdsource solutions and gain market information on crop prices. The platform received investment from a VC fund of $32 million enabling it to grow and scale to achieve greater impact addressing UN SDGs across the board.

In summary, the social tech movement, university accelerators and entrepreneurship education for graduates and lifelong learners are priorities for next generation universities seeking to achieve inclusive and sustainable wealth creation post-pandemic, achieving both economic and societal benefit.

Tipping point for an emerging next generation university

Universities have reached a threshold moment, a tipping point, and how they respond will give rise to a new type of university that embraces digitally enabled education, open innovation (research) leading to commercialisation for societal benefit through a multi-sector, challenge-oriented mission strategy. Now is the time for universities worldwide to demonstrate to their publics their value in creating transformational strategic alliances that include research, education and innovation to solve societal challenges. The incentives for this approach are far more than just securing outstanding 'impact case studies', as is increasingly important for gaining public research funding in the UK.

As global society seeks to 'build back better' post-pandemic, will universities have the vision, energy, compassion, motivation and alliance capacity to rise to the challenge and build a better world? Will they learn how to partner with others who have different organisational cultures to work together towards a common purpose? The 'pandemic mindset' to find solutions rapidly certainly led to an increased sense of goodwill and clearer priorities for universities in forming partnerships to address COVID-19. Many leading universities put aside IPR claims to accelerate collaboration.[27]

By refocusing their efforts towards a collaborative approach to addressing such challenges exemplified by the UN SDGs, they can ensure that graduates are equipped with the skills they need to succeed in today's rapidly changing world. They can create students who become globally aware citizens and recognise a moral obligation towards others.

Digital transformation has accelerated the movement towards this tipping point. It offers new technologies for connecting with people to exchange knowledge, for teaching and curriculum delivery, and for research collaboration across multidisciplinary global networks. The impact of this will be job creation and economic growth alongside positive social change.

Both interdisciplinary and transdisciplinary research and innovation is needed for social transformation. Interdisciplinary research brings together scientists from a wide variety of academic disciplines to interact, including engineers, economists, political scientists, social psychologists and behaviour change experts. Transdisciplinary research. on the other hand, has an even wider focus, delivering new concepts, insights and approaches to solving complex challenges, through scientists and stakeholders across the quintuple helix.

University collaborations with industry typically start small and are initially focused on transactional engagement through consultancy or student projects, for example. Indeed, the two can be combined through supervised consultancy, and research has shown the importance of students for growing KE.[28] It is vital for universities to demonstrate added value at this early stage, and to then look to scale the partnership by developing 'stickiness' and momentum. This will require institutional collaboration internally and capacity building to ensure that a strong partnership that is as frictionless as possible can progress.

Often the greatest barriers to collaboration can come from within the university rather than from the industry partner. Such issues include IPR and concerns about conflicts of interest and losing academic freedom and independence. While these are valid concerns, they can be easily addressed through transparent and clear communication with industry around expectations of partnerships and what success for both parties looks like. Clear governance policies and processes in place at the university also help here.

Understanding the genealogy of universities

J.G. Wissema, Professor Emeritus at the Technology University in Delft in the Netherlands, described a genealogy or typology of universities in his influential book *Towards the 3rd Generation University*.[29] 3rd and even 4th generation universities are facing major challenges adjusting to this age of rapid digital transformation, collaboration and agile working. We develop this concept further to propose that emerging 5th generation universities will have more adaptable structures and organisational cultures that value partnership for positive change. They seek to fulfil a role of being a force for good in the world by providing public benefit at different scales: locally, regionally, nationally and internationally.

Alliances are a vehicle for universities to share their resources, skills and expertise with the knowledge and reach of companies to address the key challenges of our age, transforming industry sectors and the way we live for the good of society. 5th generation universities are marked by their focus on growing transformational strategic alliances across sectors. Some of the benefits of transformational alliances compared to 3rd and 4th generation transactional and even 'strategic' relationships are shown in Table 1.3. Transformational

Table 1.3: Characteristics of transactional v transformational university–industry relationships

Transactional (3rd/4th generation)	Transformational (5th generation)
• Ad-hoc projects with local/ departmental focus • Limited forward planning for project continuation • No overarching engagement strategy • Multiple negotiations/ communications and contracting • No common metrics or key performance indicators (KPIs) captured • Lost opportunities and lack of efficiency	• Executive sponsorship • Joint business partnership steering group • Engaging and clearly defined shared purpose/mission • Strategic alliances contractual engagement process • Structured approach • Benefits include broader efficiency gains • Enables long term, themed, shared research programmes • Co-innovation culture and working practices • Co-created partnering roadmap • Transparency across collaboration activities • Simplified negotiation and contracting • Accelerated deployment of projects • Cross-departmental and faculty collaboration • Impact measurement • Use of digital technologies to improve engagement across organisations • KPIs show clear Return on Investment (ROI) with sustainable growth

strategic alliances provide 5th generation universities with significant benefits that create a step change in how they can deliver positive change at scale and pace.

Servant leadership, equality, reciprocity and the compassionate university

Now, more than ever, university leaders must demonstrate courageous servant leadership to address the greatest challenges facing the world with compassion and with all the resources of their institutions. This means actively welcoming alliance formation on equal terms with institutions from the Global South, making relationships more equitable, including between academics and professional services staff (see Table 1.1). It also means promoting greater digital inclusion and access to online higher education and creating a more inclusive, global academic system.

It is encouraging to see that prestigious science institutions like the Royal Academy of Engineering have launched an 'Africa Prize for Engineering Innovation' which awards crucial commercialisation support to ambitious African innovators developing scalable engineering solutions to local challenges[40] This demonstrates the importance of engineering as an enabler of improved quality of life and economic development in the Global South. 5th generation universities in the Global North will proactively seek to work with partners in the Global South to support building stronger innovation ecosystems that will leverage greater investment and tackle global poverty.

Professor Tawana Kupe, Vice-Chancellor and Principal of the University of Pretoria (UP) believes the pandemic is an opportunity to rethink, reimagine and reposition universities and their role in broader society to create a different and better world. In October 2021 he was awarded an honorary doctorate by the University of Montpellier for his work in 'building academic partnerships across the African continent and the globe, and for his leadership in transformation of higher education at a global level'. Under his leadership, almost 30,000 UP students are directly involved in community projects as part of their annual curriculum. Professor Kupe concluded his address with a call to the academic fraternity to:

'redouble our efforts to build equitable and sustainable partnerships, and to extend them broadly to partners in both the Global South and the Global North. No university, country or region of the world can do it alone, and this work is certainly not for ourselves, but for the very livelihood of our planet and our future generations.'[31]

Positive change transcends borders and languages. 5th generation universities will seek to co-create educational, research and innovation programmes between Global North and South through reciprocal and mutually beneficial alliances built around hybrid models of delivery. Figure 1.9 shows the potential complementary nature of Global North–South relationships. They will involve international internships, staff, and student exchange, as well as online, digitally enabled collaboration, teaching and research.

The word 'compassion' literally means 'to suffer with', and relieving suffering through education, research and innovation for social good should be the new mission of the 5th generation university.

Figure 1.9: Complementary features of Global North and Global South universities that can facilitate transformational alliances

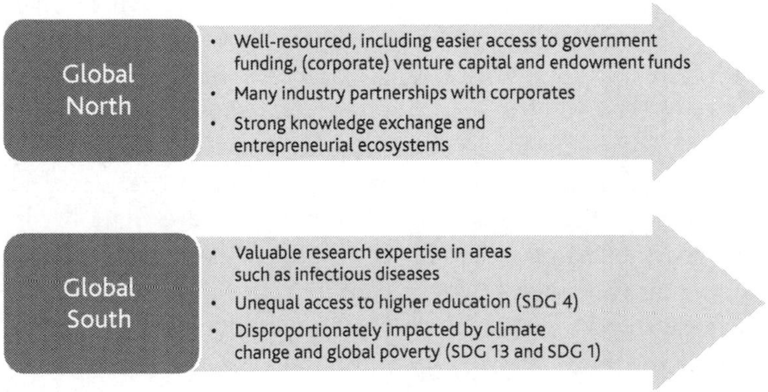

Global North
- Well-resourced, including easier access to government funding, (corporate) venture capital and endowment funds
- Many industry partnerships with corporates
- Strong knowledge exchange and entrepreneurial ecosystems

Global South
- Valuable research expertise in areas such as infectious diseases
- Unequal access to higher education (SDG 4)
- Disproportionately impacted by climate change and global poverty (SDG 13 and SDG 1)

Prioritising being the best 'for' the world, not the best 'in' the world

What kind of 'impact' should society value arising from higher education? Universities are driven by metrics such as graduate jobs created, fundraising, prestigious rankings for research outputs and others. The value of higher education needs to be reconsidered in light of the tremendous upheaval facing the world and it is encouraging to see that new impact rankings have been developed by organisations like THE (Times Higher Education) that recognise the importance of universities addressing the UN SDGs.[32] However, there is a danger that a myopic focus on metrics and rankings alone can distort the real value of higher education.

We agree with the sentiment of Assistant Professor Albert Cheng from the University of Arkansas, who states: 'we need a broader conversation about the aim of education, not just about job prospects but discerning vocation, finding formative connections ..., higher education is so much more than just one more tool in the race to get ahead'.[33]

Industry partnerships are complementary to the mission of universities by helping students gain industry experience and valuable mentors. By working together on projects related to achieving the UN SDGs, students can leave university with a deeper understanding of ethical obligations towards others, including a sense of compassion that motivates students to make a positive difference in the world. The world is now recovering and rebuilding from a devastating pandemic. Universities too must rebuild themselves to be more effective at aiding the recovery of wider society or, in other words, seeking to be the best 'for' the world that they can be rather than prioritising being the best 'in' the world through rankings.

This is a reciprocal mindset that says, 'let me help you to prosper, for our common good'. It is not about selfish gain or advancing organisational reputation, rather about a mutual win-win relationship. There is an African philosophy called 'Ubuntu' which embodies this. It is about thinking what the university can give away through complementary skills, technologies and assets to support a better tomorrow for everyone, by working in partnership towards the common good, just like that embodied in the UN SDGs. Ubuntu prioritises shared humanity across private and public life.

Working with corporates does not necessarily mean that you must be completely content with capitalism in all its forms. Rather, it means that you recognise pragmatically that the best way to achieve solutions for some of our biggest challenges is through building strategic alliances with organisations that can make real change happen at scale. Positive transformation itself is a process that is reciprocal, in which organisations are first transformed internally and then subsequently transform their environment and external partners. This is similar to the way that enlightened marriages can, through patience, perseverance, mutual learning and understanding, lead to self-transformation.

The COVID-19 outbreak from December 2019 resulted in huge disruption to society around the world, changing life as we knew it for many individuals and organisations. The university sector was disrupted on a huge scale. From 11 March 2020, the World Health Organization (WHO) declared a global pandemic. Transformational strategic alliances are vital for responding to emerging existential challenges to global development and creating a more resilient, fairer and better world.

The 5th generation university concept

Several scholars have completed literature reviews of best practices for university–industry partnerships; however often the KE practitioner's voice is not heard. Often the people, processes and governance that are vital for alliances are not considered. In our experience, this is a fatal flaw. In this book, we focus on actionable insights arising from good practices that we have tried and tested. Through attending conferences and having discussions with leading practitioners from around the world, in a variety of different contexts, we have concluded that these ingredients really work for the recipe of transformational strategic alliances.

Innovation is critical to today's business environment, even more so in the post-pandemic era where adaptability and agility are highly prized tools for success. Our conceptual model of the 5th generation university builds on our practical experience within university KE and corporate relations. We have also reviewed best practices within professional and sector-focused associations and the academic literature. We consider what are the barriers and enablers of effective and sustainable collaboration at a range of different levels, from the individual through to whole institution, with a focus on solutions.

In developing this transformative and generative model, we draw from the concept of Creating Shared Value (CSV) proposed by Michael E. Porter and Mark R. Kramer in 2006.[34] We have also been influenced by the economist of 'mission-oriented innovation', Professor Mariana Mazzucato, and innovation theorists, like Professor Dan Breznitz, who have highlighted the inequality in our current innovation processes.

Mazzucato's work highlights how 'missions' must foster multi-sector interactions and drive bottom-up solutions to global grand challenges.[35] Missions are 'concrete targets within a challenge that act as frames and stimuli for innovation'.[36] We explore the process through which 5th generation universities will contribute to both global and local (glocal) innovation.

The 5th generation university learns from and builds on the understanding of the role and practice of previous generations of universities, just as some corals in a barrier reef adapt to the effects of climate change to survive coral bleaching through producing their own kind of sunblock. Coral reefs form an intricately interdependent and interconnected ecosystem, each part contributing value to the whole.

As next generation universities from the Global North and Global South work together as part of an evolving ecosystem of research and innovation for societal benefit, along with transdisciplinary partners from industry, government and civil society, the value of the whole is far greater than the value of the individual parts. Each part has a different but complementary role. This is about equality in diversity and could be described as research, teaching and innovation 'co-valorisation'. The term 'valorisation' refers to creating, realising and releasing value through turning invention and knowledge into practice, and is complementary to 'innovation'.

In his book *Innovation in Translation: How Big Ideas Really Happen*, Dave Ferrera uses a baseball analogy to describe how team building is essential for effective innovation to occur.[37] In the next decade, increasingly led by 5th generation universities, we will see multi-sector teams working across the quintuple helix enabling greater co-innovation and co-valorisation of knowledge on an unprecedented scale.

In the field of artificial intelligence and deep learning, Deep Generative Models (DGMs) combine models of probability (generating outcomes) from input (x) and output (y) variables and deep neural networks. These neural networks have a significantly lower number of parameters than the data volume needed to train them on. This enables the models to automatically learn how to find the essence of the dataset they need to generate. In a similar manner, 5th generation universities will learn from the 'input' and 'output' data of 3rd and 4th generation universities that they have 'trained on' over their many years of experience. This ability to learn and adapt is the reason why universities have endured for many centuries. They are resilient organisations and, like a DGM, can take account of the significant few parameters that really matter in a highly volatile environment. Such parameters include responding to the following key questions:

- What is the role of universities in creating shared value (public good) for society in this era?
- How can universities leverage external resources and form alliances to co-create value most effectively?

Table 1.4 compares the characteristics of different generations of universities and lays out a clear evolutionary path towards the 5th generation university. Higher learning institutions have existed since ancient times in many cultures around the world to provide frameworks for scholars to undertake learning and research. These ancient centres are distinguished from the autonomous, degree-awarding bodies of scholars that were formed by Catholic monks in medieval Europe known by the Latin term *universitas magistrorum et scholarium*, which translates as 'community of teachers and scholars'. The first university in this sense was the University of Bologna, founded in 1088.

Table 1.4: Evolution of the university: characteristics of 1st, 2nd, 3rd, 4th and 5th generation universities

	1st generation	2nd generation	3rd generation	4th generation	5th generation
Mission/ objective	Education	Education and research	Education, research and 'third stream' know-how exploitation. KE solely focused on commercialisation (spinouts/licensing)	Education, open innovation (research), know-how exploitation, impact including through proactive economic development (GDP growth), regional engagement and regeneration	Digitally enabled education, open innovation (research) leading to commercialisation with societal benefit to promote human wellbeing. Multiple pathways for 'glocal' KE and impact.
Role	Defend truth	Discover nature	Create value	Enable value creation for societal benefit	Collaborate with quintuple helix partners to deliver transformational and sustainable value, impact, societal benefit, launch pad for disruptive and 'responsible' innovation
Method	Scholastic	Modern science/ mono-disciplinary	Modern science/ interdisciplinary, single-generational learning	Post-modern science/multi-disciplinary/multi-actor innovation	Impact driven post-modern science, transdisciplinary, multi-sector innovation particularly 'social innovation'. Transformational strategic alliances for sustainable development, seek 'collaborative' rather than 'competitive' advantage, emphasis on stewardship of important multi-sector relationships and lifelong learning.

(continued)

Table 1.4: Evolution of the university: characteristics of 1st, 2nd, 3rd, 4th and 5th generation universities (continued)

	1st generation	2nd generation	3rd generation	4th generation	5th generation
Output	Professionals	Professionals and scientists	Professionals, scientists and entrepreneurs	Professionals, scientists, entrepreneurs and competitive local economy (artists, customers, ecosystem participants)	Professionals, scientists, entrepreneurs and leaders of multi-sector transformational strategic alliances to achieve positive change and contribute towards UN SDGs
Language	Latin	National	English	Multilingual (National and English)	Multilingual (National and English)
Organisation	Colleges	Faculties	Institutes and centres	Innovation spaces	Integration, orchestration and streamlining of research, teaching and innovation across organisation. Digital, transdisciplinary and multi-sector aligned co-innovation spaces
Management	Chancellor	Part-time academics	Professional management, hierarchical	Professional management and local experts/Disruptors	Digitally aware, collaborative professional management, disruptors, innovative leaders and social reformers
Orientation	Universal	National	Global	Ecosystem	Glocal
Alliance approach	Almost non-existent	Ad-hoc	Transactional and philanthropic	Tactical and strategic, market competing	Quicker to create multi-sector, peer-to-peer, collaborative, transformational, market and shared value-creating, partner selection critical
Emergence	11th century	1800s	2000s	2010s	2020s

Source: Adapted from Wissema (2009),[38] Lukovics and Zuti (2013)[39]

Western style universities have transitioned from their foundation in monastic communities about a millennium ago to become the living, connective tissue of the knowledge economy. We argue that now they must become the fuel for the wellbeing or 'impact economy'.

In the early 2010s we believe that 4th generation universities started to emerge, seeking significantly higher mutual value in their relationships with external partners. In the UK, Cambridge scholar Tomas Coates Ulrichsen noted a key trend identified in the Higher Education Innovation Fund (HEIF) 2011–15 strategies of universities in England towards a desire to form longer-term, strategic alliances with external users 'providing a more coherent and cohesive approach to their business engagement'.[40] He referred to the Universities of Exeter and Manchester:

> The University of Exeter argues that this has led to more referrals and repeat business for the institution. The University of Manchester notes that these types of holistic and strategic partnerships have the potential not only to secure longer-term funding for research, but also bring benefits for student and graduate employability, internships, and entrepreneurship.

In contrast to previous generations, 5th generation universities will move beyond seeing a university's core activities as being research and teaching, plus a 'third mission' mainly seen as research commercialisation and technology transfer. Instead, they have fully integrated research, teaching and innovation in their curriculums and institutional strategies. They have a broader concept of public benefit and the common good underpinning a forward-thinking approach to alliances. They see relationship with external organisations, through innovation ecosystems, as a core strategic asset and a catalyst for the move towards the creation of a more ethical capitalism. They recognise the importance of non-academic, professional 'knowledge brokers' in externally facing roles, engaging with partners in industry, government and civil society, speaking to them in a non-academic language. 5th generation universities recognise that the SDGs are political and not value-neutral, they speak about a better world for everyone.

5th generation universities have evolved to see 'commercialisation' as a non-linear and multifaceted innovation process that is far more than just spinout creation, licensing or attracting investment. Rather, it is about adding value to multidisciplinary knowledge creation or co-production across the academic–industry–civil society nexus through a purpose- or mission-driven approach, for example to achieve objectives like the UN SDGs. Figure 1.10 shows how such knowledge valorisation involves technological as well as organisational innovation and transformation (positive change).

Figure 1.10: How 5th generation universities partner and co-innovate to achieve their institutional vision, shared objectives and transformation, both within the university and externally

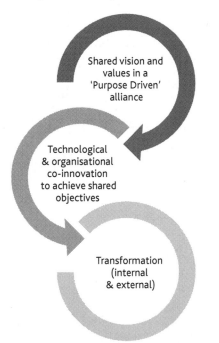

In considering how 5th generation universities and their transformational strategic alliances can help solve the complex problems facing the world today, our focus is more on effective execution and implementation than theory.

Value co-creation in 5th generation universities

Value creation is an innovative, collaborative and generative process, generally building on 'slow hunches' rather than sudden breakthroughs, to quote Steven Johnson in his book *Where Good Ideas Come From*.[41] Value is generated when universities and industry co-create knowledge (discover) and develop collaborative innovation processes that focus on shared goals, for example to achieve societal benefit by tackling the UN SDGs. The 5th generation university will learn how to effectively co-create value through forming transformational strategic alliances. This will lead to a positive feedback loop, as shown in Figure 1.11 where there is sufficient critical mass through multi-sector engagement and collaboration to release huge amounts of impact. The exact industries or technology areas that are the focus of a 5th generation university's alliances will vary depending on each university's capabilities, interests and expertise, as well as their geographical and socio-economic context to a certain extent.

How is value co-creation managed through transformational strategic alliances that focus on the SDGs? Structured frameworks

Figure 1.11: The positive feedback loop of transformational strategic alliances, through co-valorisation (shared value creation) and positive change (impact)

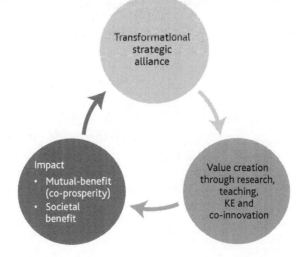

such as OKR (objectives and key results) can certainly help to plan and measure the value and impact from collaboration, by ensuring that objectives align rather than diverge, and key results are captured. It is remarkable in our experience how often a simple cost-benefit analysis is missed out in planning for alliances. This analysis enables an assessment of complementary assets and resources that both parties bring to the table and combine to create value greater than the sum of their parts. Objectives must always seek to add value for both sides as well as for wider society to achieve success.

Alliances require clear goals and the right combination of people at different levels in organisations to implement them. This is a deep learning process. Poor planning and management are often the greatest barriers to forming transformational strategic alliances.

Post-pandemic, it remains to be seen how important travel and face-to-face contact with collaborators will be in forming trusted relationships that deliver mutual-benefit and create shared value. We expect that a blended approach, involving mainly online video conferencing for initial discussions with companies followed by face-to-face contact once the relationship has developed, is likely to become the norm in future.

Recovering faster in a post-pandemic knowledge economy moving towards zero carbon

Effective university–industry alliances can help society to recover more quickly from the damage caused by the pandemic. 5th generation universities will have learned from the rapid digital transformation required in pivoting to a more digital and inclusive academic environment in response to the global lockdowns of 2020 and 2021. Exactly how local and national economies can be revitalised following the pandemic will be a hot topic among many governments. A combination of triple, quadruple and quintuple helix-aware alliances can power up governments' industrial strategies and accelerate a transition to a much cleaner and greener planet. This transition to tackle the 'climate emergency' (SDG 13) is a much greater challenge facing the world than the recent pandemic.

The climate emergency is a planetary-scale existential threat affecting whole ecosystems. The period we are living in is now known as the Anthropocene due to rapidly worsening climate and biodiversity loss directly related to human impact on the planet. Biodiversity is declining faster than at any time in human history. Since 1970, there has been a 68 per cent decline in the populations of mammals, birds, fish, reptiles and amphibians. Currently, scientists believe that one million animal and plant species, about a quarter of the global total, are threatened with extinction.[42]

In 2017, the Carbon Majors Report, produced by a non-profit organisation Carbon Disclosure Project (CDP) in collaboration with the Climate Accountability Institute, claimed that just 100 companies are responsible for 71 per cent of global greenhouse gas emissions since 1988, the year the Intergovernmental Panel on Climate Change was established.[43] The report was compiled from publicly available emissions figures. It clearly highlighted the role that companies, and their investors, could play in addressing climate change. Pedro Faria, the report's author was reported in *The Guardian* as saying that the barrier to companies changing is the 'absolute tension' between short-term thinking around profits and the urgent need to reduce emissions.[44]

Should universities seek to form transformational strategic alliances with energy companies? Each institution must decide based on a mixture of moral and ethical values and pragmatism. Any university focused on partnerships must have a robust due-diligence process in place to decide on the suitability of any alliance for their organisation. The utilitarian or pragmatic response may be that the greatest impact on climate change could be achieved by transforming these companies and industries towards more sustainable business models based around renewable energy technologies rather than fossil fuels. Increasingly, investors are realising that fossil fuel investments do not make business sense and the energy companies themselves know that they need to make big changes to their business models.[45] There is growing pressure from wider society for such companies to demonstrate their focus on sustainability in a rapidly changing world.

Many multinational technology corporates such as Apple, Facebook and Google have committed to 100 per cent renewable power under the RE100 initiative.[46] As previously mentioned, the social tech investor community are also starting to focus on more sustainable practices with both a positive impact on society and return on investment for shareholders. For example, many governments are mandating all-electric vehicle sales by as early as 2030. This will have a huge impact not only on the automotive industry, but also on manufacturing and other sectors such as construction, architecture and urban design.

The marketisation of higher education and the role of universities in promoting a more equitable world may not necessarily conflict. It makes business sense for universities to focus on the UN SDGs, as surveys show that students are attracted to institutions with strong, social justice values.[47] Generation Z, those who make up most of the current student population, are keen to create solutions for greater societal benefit and are attracted to universities and employers who have the same attitude and commitment.

Co-innovation for shared value creation

Princeton Professor David MacMillan was jointly awarded a Nobel Prize in chemistry in 2021, 'for the development of asymmetric organocatalysis', designing and building small organic molecules to propel chemical reactions, with many potentially beneficial societal applications in healthcare and other fields.[48] Professor MacMillan spoke about the importance of partnership with industry in his work and how his university seeks to achieve both excellence in research and societal good. In tributes from colleagues, he was described as 'a true entrepreneurial scholar, innovating both in the lab and through the creation of new ventures and collaborations with industry to translate complex research findings into tangible benefits for society'.[49]

Effective external engagement with industry partners through transformational alliances is a key capability that many universities are currently lacking. Universities need to find a common language with industry collaborators around joint value creation for social good and mutual benefit. They need to understand the needs of industry for disruptive as well as just incremental innovation, around decarbonisation for example, and present a vision of how university collaborative assets can complement and advance the company's innovation efforts through joint projects. This is co-innovation for shared value creation.

The 5th generation university achieves the greatest co-value creation (both mutual and societal benefit) through the closest alignment of values (institutional values of the university and ethical business priorities of the corporates) between partners (Figure 1.12). In a multifaceted transformational strategic alliance, 5th generation universities will find solutions to complex global challenges such as the UN SDGs, and deliver at scale through multi-sector engagements, offering positive change for the world. These alliances lead and redefine both the higher education and industry sectors involved, often through disruptive innovation.

Through strategic alliances, 4th generation universities may deliver new-to-market, breakthrough innovation, though without a deep, long-term transformational alliance, there is not the necessary critical mass and energy to deliver solutions at scale. 3rd generation universities from the 2000s mainly deliver incremental (new-to-company) innovation through transactional partnerships involving contract research or consultancy for example.

Figure 1.12. How 3rd, 4th and 5th generation universities approach value alignment and co-value creation

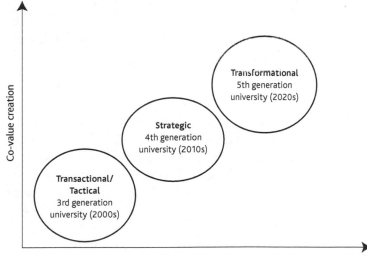

A blended approach to alliances adopted by 5th generation universities

Universities must be able to clearly demonstrate mutual benefit to corporates with a blended approach encompassing both programmatic and philanthropic aspects. Soon, this will enable leading corporates of the world to collaborate with universities that are integrated and have a transformational strategic approach to external engagement. This collaborative and symbiotic approach will paradoxically help corporates and universities to retain their competitive edge (this is termed 'co-opetition'), hence achieving a quicker Return on Investment (ROI), in terms of both financial and societal benefit.

Author Nik Miller from fundraising consultancy More Partnership writes:

> Corporate partners aren't cash machines; they are much more useful than that. Engaged thoughtfully, they can make transformative contributions to societal causes through partnership working. For commercially minded, judicious and adaptable professionals in the cultural, charitable and university sectors, the undefined boundaries of corporate collaborations and promise of deep impact are an alluring prospect.[50]

Open innovation and entrepreneurial ecosystems driven by 5th generation universities

Rankings drive competition, so what drives cooperation and collaboration? The market is driving major companies to focus more on open innovation than ever before and building trust and resilience through delivering social good. The open innovation economy is fuelling convergence of different technology areas across sectors and disciplines. The creation of 'innovation districts' is an attempt to harness, orchestrate and advance convergence of economic, physical and networking assets within a small area where quadruple helix organisations can interact and collaborate. It is a place-based model of innovation, often, though not exclusively, focused on new campus developments or research parks.

In our experience working with local government and economic development, the innovation and problem-solving 'firepower' of universities is greatly underrecognised and underutilised to address societal challenges. When a road needs fixing, councils are used to forming long-term supplier partnerships with companies. When a seaside town needs regenerating, councils see the value of public art in attracting and boosting tourism and the visitor economy. However, when there are pressing societal, economic and environmental challenges facing a locality, how often do local governments consider forming alliances with universities or facilitating local businesses to work more closely with universities? Very rarely. This is not only to the detriment of the knowledge economy in the region, but talent is also being wasted and revolutionary social innovation that could come from the 'engine room' of universities working through multi-sector alliances is not being tapped into.

Mapping tool to support 5th generation university planning to tackle United Nations Sustainable Development Goals

Table 1.5 illustrates how a 5th generation university may plan programmatic activities to target solutions that tackle each of the UN SDGs in a holistic and multifaceted manner. Goal 17 underpins the whole approach so there is a focus on forming transformational strategic alliances across all sectors in the quintuple helix ecosystem.

Table 1.5: Examples of how 5th generation universities may tackle different UN SDGs in an integrated and holistic manner

UN SDG	Examples of 5th generation university activity
1) End poverty	Creation of jobs through setting up a social purpose-driven, technology and entrepreneurship accelerator both locally in your university region and then building capacity to scale such centres nationally and internationally to help resource the Global South
2) Zero hunger	Research and co-innovation activity focused on AgTech to improve agricultural productivity, food security, resilience and nutritional value
3) Global health and wellbeing	Setting up a centre of excellence for digital innovation in healthcare working with quadruple helix partners including clinicians and regulators to scale production of affordable medicines, diagnostics, sensors, vaccines, and drug delivery
4) Quality education	Development and glocal roll-out of affordable, accessible, and inclusive lifelong learning and educational resources for teaching higher education curriculums across academic disciplines and involving guest lecturers from industry and civil society
5) Gender equality	Achieving equality of representation and income for all gender identities across industries, thereby improving opportunities
6) Clean water and sanitation	Development of water purification and filtration technologies and processes that are affordable and appropriate for people in different regions. This will involve a strong focus on frugal innovation processes and circular-economy thinking
7) Affordable and clean energy	Development of environmentally sustainable, affordable, reliable clean energy sources including both storage and use within a circular economy and integrating frugal innovation approaches
8) Decent work and economic growth	Reskilling and job creation through providing affordable and accessible higher education and training in entrepreneurship through university accelerators, particularly with a social innovation focus, targeting the impact investment community

(continued)

Table 1.5: Examples of how 5th generation universities may tackle different UN SDGs in an integrated and holistic manner (continued)

UN SDG	Examples of 5th generation university activity
9) Industry, innovation and infrastructure	Setting up novel entrepreneurship accelerators and research centres through transformational alliances with local and regional governments to help to 'level up', reduce inequalities and create new opportunities for all
10) Reduced inequalities	Achieving equality of representation and salaries for all diversity groups across industries; reducing inequality globally by growing educational partnerships between Global North and Global South
11) Sustainable cities and communities	Setting targets and working towards becoming a zero-carbon campus, working closely with local and regional governments to bring transformative change in the way that resources are used
12) Responsible consumption and production	Ensuring responsible consumption and production of goods on campus and incentivising social scientists and behaviour change experts to work with industry to nudge civil society towards more responsible consumption habits
13) Climate action	A UK university may harness investment for sustainability initiatives by offering a sustainability (ESG benchmark) bond to financial markets that will provide long-term funding for effective environmental, social and governance initiatives
14) Life below water	Developing novel materials and solutions for marine conservation including tackling plastic waste through research, innovation and knowledge exchange
15) Life on land	Policy engagement to highlight the importance of materials and methods to ensure the sustainability of land-based biodiversity and ecosystems
16) Peace, justice, and strong institutions	Promotion of effective, equitable, inclusive and accountable institutions and societies through effective policy engagement that leverages multi-disciplinary academic expertise
17) Partnership for the goals	Implementing and supporting glocal strategic alliances between researchers in the public, private and voluntary sector to facilitate the transition to a zero-carbon and 'wellbeing' economy

Case study: How a transformational strategic alliance approach was applied to corporate engagement and philanthropy for a new campus development

This case study illustrates how a leading, research-intensive UK university incorporated a novel approach to forming transformational strategic alliances with industry stakeholders. This was based around the need to engage corporates to build capacity for a new campus.

A transformational strategic alliance takes a long-term, blended programmatic and philanthropic approach to changing sectoral practice through cutting-edge technology, improved operations and responsible innovation that can contribute to the UN SDGs. The university's approach was to develop a place-based alliance with the most valued corporates at the new campus. The campus development itself provided a unique opportunity to develop a multidisciplinary, knowledge-based ecosystem for open innovation to solve pressing issues such as how to remove plastic waste from the world's oceans.

The alliance professionals involved stated the importance of active listening to corporates to recognise and value the experience, skills and reach that the industry brings, creating the potential to truly transform industry sectors through collaboration in research and development.

The alliance team helped corporates to navigate the university's multidisciplinary academic expertise and resources by acting as a single point of contact or interface with the university. They explained how the new campus would enable the university to achieve greater impact than ever before. They maintained effective, regular internal and external communication alongside utilising a CRM system to record all interactions with stakeholders.

The alliance team demonstrated the ability to influence senior academics without having direct line-management responsibility, to meet with relevant companies and discuss opportunities for long-term collaboration rooted in shared vision and values. They showed their strong communication, interpersonal and diplomatic skills to broker robust peer-to-peer relationships between academic and industry leaders. Above all, they highlighted the importance of trusted relationships that take time to build.

The team discussed the need to gather corporate intelligence prior to any meeting. This involved reviewing investor reports, for example, to discover areas of interest and consider how those areas aligned with the university's campus plans. The team mentioned that a structured approach to corporate engagement is very helpful for industry partners, so they know what to expect in future interactions.

The alliance directors acted as facilitators, moving conversations from exploration to action, working with the corporate representatives to develop mutually beneficial projects within a collaborative strategic framework. In addition to small group or one to-one meetings, they were also able to organise 'town hall'-style meetings, bringing together research leaders across multiple research disciplines to focus on a specific area.

The team developed a bespoke proposal for the corporate for potential programmatic and philanthropic areas of engagement. They sought internal buy-in and validation of this proposal to ensure there were academic champions or executive sponsors internally before presenting the proposal to the corporate.

As trusted relationships evolved, there were often several visits to campus highlighting technology demonstrators that illustrated the capabilities of the university academics and attracted further interest. Meetings often covered both technology and talent pipeline opportunities for industry to engage with academics. This benefits-focused approach was welcomed by industry. The team also ensured that conversations covered both mutual benefits as well as potential societal benefits of collaboration, for example addressing grand challenge themes. Figure 1.13 provides an overview of the structured approach these alliance professionals took.

Lessons learned

• There is a need and huge potential for both academia and industry to align university vision, mission and strategy around global grand challenges such as the UN SDGs to achieve global societal benefit. Many university vision and mission statements already have ambitious aspirations to achieve societal benefit. The SDGs are not a perfect blueprint

Figure 1.13: The transformative strategic alliance journey, from initial workshop to added-value transformational outputs

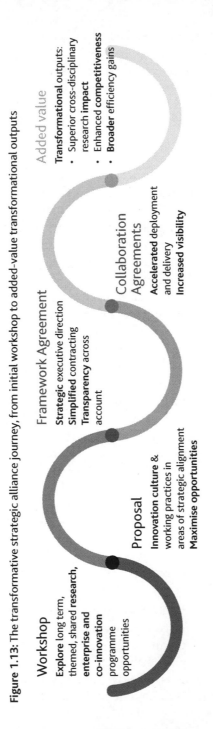

Workshop

Explore long term, themed, shared **research, enterprise and co-innovation** programme opportunities

Proposal

Innovation culture & working practices in areas of strategic alignment **Maximise opportunities**

Framework Agreement

Strategic executive direction
Simplified contracting
Transparency across account

Collaboration Agreements

Accelerated deployment and delivery
Increased visibility

Added value

Transformational outputs:
• Superior cross-disciplinary research **impact**
• Enhanced **competitiveness**
• **Broader** efficiency gains

of an ideal world, but they are a great start and can help universities to accelerate their progress towards realising their vision and mission.

- Ambitious and transformational collaborative alliances have a critical role in KE and the co-valorisation of research and teaching. The growing importance of cross-disciplinary KE is recognised by governments in both the Global North and the Global South and this requires impactful alliances between people and organisations.

- Impact is defined as building long-term, trusted two-way, sustainable, trans-disciplinary relationships with industry that do social good and align with institutional values.

- It is important to inspire, motivate and equip practitioners from multiple sectors to see the value of co-innovation and enable transformational alliances to solve global challenges.

- During the darkest days of the pandemic, governments, industry and civil society have seen a demonstration of the impact of KE and collaboration with universities for social good, through rapid vaccine and medical developments.

- A precedent has been set in facing COVID-19 for accelerating collaborative partnerships that will 'think big' to tackle other pressing societal challenges, such as climate change and fast-track co-developed solutions exponentially through an integrated quintuple helix approach to collaboration.

- Alliance and KE professionals in universities are an often unseen, underestimated, undervalued and unrecognised group who are skilled at harnessing the power of alliances for widespread socioeconomic benefit. Universities must rediscover their public good role and empower and retain these professionals so they can help to strengthen resilience in the post-pandemic era and deliver greater impact from their research, KE and teaching.

- Universities are constantly evolving to adjust to their changing environments. The 5th generation university is a result of rapid changes in the external political, economic, and social environment, accelerated by the pandemic, that have inspired changes in the function and form of universities.

- Wise university leaders with foresight will change their organisational thinking and collaborative practices to adjust to both systemic and existential threats and opportunities, such as climate change, digital transformation and Industry 4.0.

- A holistic approach to collaboration will enable universities to organise their activities to deliver outstanding public benefit and to maximise opportunities to impact positively on their regions, locally, nationally and internationally. The key is to offer a comprehensive holistic framework covering both programmatic activities and philanthropic/ fundraising considerations.

- Traditional linear models of university–industry interactions rely on building strategic alliances from initial short-term transactional projects. However, these models do not take account of the benefits for both parties in starting relationships with greater mutual awareness and partner selection and a long-term ambition to co-innovate to address the urgent challenges facing the world today. In such non-linear relationships, trust can build more quickly when the relationship is framed through a more mature strategic intent from both parties.

- Strategic alliance functionality within a university or industry, whatever their R&D context, becomes a source of 'transformational collaborative advantage' helping these organisations proactively shape their environments in an age of rapid social and economic change and move beyond competing.

- To develop our transformative, generative and non-linear model, a fresh concept of co-value creation through 'mission-oriented innovation' and transformational strategic alliances is required. This is the 5th generation university that learns from and builds on the comprehension of the role and practice of previous generations of universities, just as some corals in a barrier reef adapt to the effects of climate change to survive coral bleaching, through producing their own kind of sunblock.

2

Enabling an environment for transformational strategic alliances

'We must halt carbon emissions this decade. We must recapture billions of tonnes of carbon from the air. We must fix our sights of keeping 1.5 degrees in reach. A new industrial revolution powered by millions of sustainable innovations is essential and is indeed already beginning.'

Sir David Attenborough's speech
at COP26 summit, October 2021

Our planetary environment, the world on which we live, has finite, precious resources. Nature is a key ally that we all benefit from. The Earth's ecosystems that are held together by a multitude of symbiotic, mutually beneficial relationships are becoming increasingly unstable. The way we live must change for the benefit of all creatures, including ourselves. One way to achieve this is for the world's universities to strengthen relationships within their ecosystems, locally, regionally, and internationally, to help build a better, more equal world together, with a reduced environmental footprint. 5th generation universities will be more ambitious in setting up deep, transformational collaborations with a wide variety of sectors and organisations that they have not worked with before to achieve better, more sustainable solutions to the world's biggest challenges. Indeed, we have argued in Chapter 1 that a transformational alliance approach focused on achieving the UN SDGs will be the defining feature of a 5th generation university.

Universities need to develop a comprehensive corporate engagement strategy covering research, teaching, and innovation or KE. They must consider how engagement across diverse sectors of the quadruple helix more generally will contribute to achieving their institutional mission, vision and values. In this chapter, we consider workforce development, student engagement, leadership strategy and how forward-thinking senior leaders can create a different culture that encourages alliances to grow. We also discuss further how 5th generation universities will be transformational: how they will transform their institutions' culture, talent (increasing diversity and inclusion), leadership, teaching and learning, impact and research.

Before we can consider why universities should engage in multi-sector transformational strategic alliances, at a range of different levels, it is important first to consider: 'What is the role of a university?' These are common answers to that question, in our experience:

- education – to equip people with knowledge, skills and experience;
- research – to create and disseminate knowledge;
- innovation and economic development;
- contributing to the public or 'common' good;
- discovery of truth and wisdom;
- achieving transformational change to make the world a better place;
- demonstrating thought leadership;
- creating work-ready graduates;
- producing globally aware, more considerate citizens.

Leaders of 5th generation universities will have the strategic thinking needed to stimulate a more ethical, market-creating innovation mindset that will see collaboration with the Global South universities as vital for achieving solutions to the UN SDGs. Their thinking is driven by opportunities for creating a better world for all and achieving greater public good through their institutions rather than achieving competitive advantage among their peers.

Objectives and key results of 5th generation universities

What goals drive your partnerships? In a good marriage, those goals are, for many of you, your happiness, and the happiness of your spouse. In other words, mutual happiness. You may also hope that through your marriage you will contribute to a better society, for example by raising children. When relationships face challenging times, if the trust and commitment remain strong from both sides, they can weather any storm. Between organisations, alliances are developed for different goals, though ultimately should seek mutual benefit and the 'common good' of society.

Before you can answer the question of what objectives should drive your university alliances, you first need to agree internally with your staff, students and wider ecosystem what your university vision and mission should be. If you see universities only as a driver of the 'knowledge economy', creating jobs and upskilling the labour market will be the most important drivers for your alliances. There is a trend for governments to see the purpose of higher education mainly in these instrumentalist terms. For local government, the civic or place-based role of a university in their region is often emphasised, in driving economic development and raising social mobility. However, while universities are often one of the large economic anchor institutions within their regions, as philanthropist Gerald Chan has argued: 'Society in fact will be short-changed if we reframe the university's mission to be about human resources rather than about humanity, and that, in the broadest sense of the word.'[1]

5th generation universities will rediscover the civic role of their institutions with a strong understanding of their place-based context and how they can contribute to positive change in their regions, addressing both societal and economic challenges such as how to create a zero-carbon economy and a more resilient future, both locally and globally. The evidence or 'key results' demonstrates that this civic role is being achieved is whether all university staff feel recognised, rewarded and incentivised to engage with KE and valorisation activities that lead to positive change in their local areas.

tandem across the institution in a coordinated manner. This is not about centralisation or decentralisation, being top-down or bottom-up in approach, rather it is combining the best of both approaches to achieve the greatest institutional progress. This is achieved through creating a culture that empowers staff to make decisions rather than to always ask permission.

Barriers to alliances

Building transdisciplinary alliances for positive change is complex. Frequent barriers that you will encounter with university–industry alliances are shown in Table 2.2. 5th generation universities will look to be flexible and find common ground to overcome barriers.

How can your university make it easier for industry partners to collaborate? First, it is vital to have the right people with the right attitude and skills on both sides to engage effectively, being fully supported by executive sponsorship. This sponsorship provides the necessary 'air cover' for these relationships to thrive. We discuss this in more detail in Chapter 3. A simple tip, though, is to ensure that your institution's contracting process is as frictionless as possible. Workflow automation, including use of digital signatures, can help accelerate and scale contracting processes to make it easier to get projects under way in a shorter timescale. Likewise, shortening non-disclosure agreements (NDAs) and framework agreements can be a useful way to speed up the process of getting legal sign-off for collaboration. At times, there will need to be a compromise to find joint solutions, and so learning to manage the expectations of both academics and industry is an important skill for those who work on developing and managing alliances. We will return to this in the next chapter.

The importance of alignment

What is alignment and why is it so important for university–industry alliances particularly? Academics see time in terms of academic terms and years, industry in terms of business quarters and fiscal years. Universities and industry therefore need to find alignment between the rhythm of academic and commercial

Table 2.2: Academic and industry barriers to alliances

Academic barriers	Industry barriers
Poor accessibility and availability of academics	Commercial timeframes related to fiscal year, or lack of flexibility to work around academic timetable
Poor organisation, planning and management, and no cost-benefit consideration	Poor organisation, planning and management, and sometimes too much focus on cost-benefit consideration without recognising the intangible benefits of working with academia
Egos and anti-corporate sentiment	Lack of understanding of academic culture or charitable status of some universities
Misaligned/diverging objectives, e.g. corporates may be seen as 'cash cows'	Mis-aligned/diverging objectives, e.g. transactional, commercially driven, with lack of concern regarding university vision, mission and values, including the need for universities to demonstrate societal benefit
Lack of resources, including specific alliance function, lead negotiator, executive champion or specialist legal and contracting support	Lack of resources, including specific alliance function, deal manager or executive champion
Institutional/regulatory frameworks including around intellectual property (IP), e.g. if the university has charitable status	Inflexible and restrictive IP ownership requirements for funded projects
Lack of understanding of commercialisation of intellectual property, e.g. patent licensing and spinout creation to start-up/scale-up ecosystem resulting in undervaluing or overvaluing assets	Lack of understanding of academic priorities and the expectations universities often have around the need to publish and to open-source IP, or the concern to protect academic freedom
Need to publish for career promotion within academia as university rankings are mainly judged on research	Need to see demonstrators of actual products, proof of concepts or prospect for co-innovation to establish credibility and delivery capacity of the university

cycles. University–industry alliances must align goals, visions and timeframes.

5th generation universities are transparent and easy to collaborate with. They are highly responsive in their communications with the outside world, adapting their language when necessary to foster mutual understanding. In a rapidly changing world, they realise the importance of 'now' rather than 'not yet'. They are compassionate, progressive and committed to making the world a better place. They have clear, fair and workable intellectual property (IP) terms for industry. They offer flexibility and adaptability and understand the requirements and R&D timescales of different industry sectors. For example, the pharmaceutical sector has lengthy clinical trials prior to product development whereas heavy manufacturing, materials science and computer technology have shorter time horizons.

In short, the next generation of universities will be able to align with the strategic priorities and interests of industry partners and create win–win benefits for all parties. This requires effective communication and negotiation, particularly in the early stages of alliances, and for the alliance teams to work closely with legal and research contracts colleagues to structure collaborations well from the outset. It is important to be clear on the amount of time that academics can commit to projects. It is always best to under-promise and over-deliver rather than over-promise and under-deliver. This approach will ensure that you build greater trust with your partners for a successful alliance.

Partner selection for these relationships should generally not be ad hoc and reactive. For instance, just because an academic has a neighbour who is a senior R&D lead in a company, it does not necessarily mean that there is a good case for their university to form a strategic alliance. Serendipity can sometimes help to initiate relationships although it is better to have an idea of your ideal partner before you start to look to engage with industry. For example, universities often have a due-diligence process in place, and so may not work with tobacco, defence or oil and gas companies.

What does your ideal alliance partner profile look like? If you are interested in securing significant philanthropic income, for example, finding corporates of sufficient scale with a track record of large gifts to universities will be a priority. Alignment to shared values can help supercharge any relationship, but this is even more the case for university–industry alliances.

Academic leaders should have research topics in mind that they would like to work on with companies who share a commitment to the institutional mission, vision and values of their university. Alongside an interest in working together on the UN SDGs, this may include a strong commitment to diversity and inclusion, or work-based student projects and student entrepreneurship.

Next you need to consider alignment of competencies in your collaborative teams, for example, blue-sky thinkers and pragmatists, starters and finishers. We recommend that realistic milestones and deliverables are included in your Collaboration Agreement's Statement of Work (SoW). You should allow time for organisational learning about how both parties think and discuss how you can communicate and engage most effectively in line with different organisational cultures. In our experience, collaborations are therefore normally most productive several months into the relationship. While it is important to think about 'quick wins' that are often transactional benefits of collaboration, it is better to have a longer-term mindset and engagement plan in place to secure a more productive and sustainable alliance.

5th generation universities will often line up around the preferred funding mechanism and expectations of industry. This means that rather than desiring unrestricted philanthropic gifts from the start of a relationship, they recognise the business and commercial imperatives of industry in building an alliance and are more flexible on funding types. Generally, industry prefers to support pre-competitive, more basic, fundamental research through philanthropic donations (gift funding, open-source and mainly unrestricted). However, more applied research and development at a higher Technology Readiness Level (TRL) is normally funded directly as sponsored research with more commercial IP and licensing terms. You could say that such work has a higher Commercial Readiness Level (CRL) and therefore is also likely to have shorter timeframes for delivery.

Figure 2.1 highlights that there are two major pathways by which universities approach industry and vice versa. Typically, universities prioritise gaining philanthropy from corporate

Figure 2.1: Major pathways and competing priorities for university–industry alliances

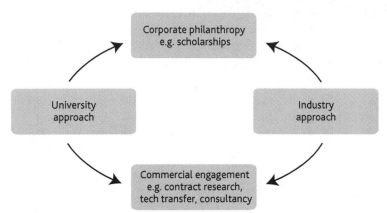

partnerships too early in the relationship. This is often driven by advancement (philanthropy) teams within academic institutions, and may hinder the development of a strategic alliance. In the long run, building a trusted relationship with the corporate will offer significantly more value for the university than simply a one-off cash donation.

In most cases, corporates initiate relationships with universities in a transactional or tactical manner, and so are more interested in programmatic activities such as contract research and talent acquisition. The challenge is to move existing relationships towards a strategic and transformational alliance that involves both programmatic and philanthropic activity. 5th generation universities will adopt a holistic approach, embracing both programmatic (generally led by corporate engagement professionals), and then philanthropic activities once a trusted relationship has been established. This approach will deliver far greater impact.

We have found that only a few large technology companies start with unrestricted philanthropic donations to establish early collaboration, as they have the appropriate scale and resources to be able to do so. They use such gift funding to assess alignment of universities with their business interests. They wish to assess how easy it is to work with different universities and use unrestricted gifts to start to build trust with academia. They also wish to discover the ability of universities to deliver results to time and budget.

We advise looking for partners who have a highly collaborative rather than transactional culture of innovation that values longer-term alliances over short-term engagements. Universities that have a more 'bottom-up' institutional culture should seek similar organisations to partner with as otherwise they are likely to experience significant collaboration challenges. However, unless 'bottom-up' universities have a strong centralised signposting function for external relations, industry can sometimes experience difficulties in finding the most appropriate contact point in a timely manner.

A holistic and integrated university approach to engaging corporates

University leaders with foresight move beyond thinking about the need to get wealthy private donors and industrialists to black-tie fundraising dinners for their philanthropy and advancement campaigns. Instead, they see universities and their leadership role more holistically with a focus on corporate engagement and not just corporate philanthropy.

Black-tie dinners may work for high-net-worth individuals and alumni, but for valued industry partners, 5th generation universities will have a more enlightened approach to fundraising. They will seek to shape proposals 'with', not 'for', industry partners, who are valued for their shared values and not just their financial support. Such university leaders will seek to venture into partnership with those from a variety of different sectors to address societal challenges together, to fulfil their institutional missions and to provide mutual benefit. In short, they will develop a long-term, sustainable relationship with their partners on a more equitable basis. This is about the co-creation of value based around shared objectives. Value ripples out from co-creation like a pebble falling into a pond when universities and industry collaborate on shared goals for wide societal benefit.

Purdue University repositioned their approach to university–industry collaborations during the pandemic to maximise their engagement through a more holistic approach. They formed a more centralised corporate partnerships team to gain a better understanding of the landscape of industry relationships on their campus, particularly who their core partners were for delivering impact. They sought to broaden their corporate engagements beyond sponsored research and philanthropy to include co-location, workforce development, entrepreneurship activity and technology transfer. In all their engagements their strategy was to align their own assets with external partners to achieve mutual benefit and a return on investment.[4]

In developing a strategy for philanthropy, building strategic alliances for the good of humanity through the UN SDGs should be considered. Some philanthropic funders love interaction with leading scientists and clinicians as they have a passion for good science. 5th generation universities empower their advancement teams to choreograph interactions with corporates that have a track record of philanthropic support towards universities. They do this in full communication and interaction with the institution's corporate engagement teams, who may already have existing relationships with those companies. In general, never be quick to ask for philanthropic funding. Universities need to be patient and demonstrate the value that they can bring to helping companies achieve their aspirations related to achieving the UN SDGs through their business activities.

Corporates have an array of assets, beyond merely financial, that they can offer through alliances, including data, network and expertise, that can achieve a combined asset far greater than cash alone. In fact, high-net-worth individuals are more likely to give more in purely financial terms as cash donation gifts to universities, so it is not healthy to see industry as a 'cash cow' for the university. Wise university leaders and alliance staff understand their organisational assets and how these can both complement and connect with external organisations to achieve shared outcomes and added value. Corporate leaders also want more from their university alliances than annual philanthropic stewardship reports and their company's name on a funding wall or building.

Strategic corporate philanthropy is becoming more sophisticated, with a strong focus on impact measurement. Porter and Kramer argue that: 'Corporations can use their charitable efforts to improve their competitive context – to enhance context brings social and economic goals into alignment and improves a company's long-term business prospects.'[5]

However, companies today are increasingly mission-driven to solve societal challenges and their contribution goes beyond 'charitable efforts' and a simple understanding of 'corporate social responsibility' (CSR) to become central to their core business strategy. Historically, this approach is nothing new. Simon Rogerson, CEO and Co-Founder of Octopus, a certified B Corporation,[6] writes:

> If you ever want a case history in how to build a great company, the history of the Cadbury business is a good place to start. It was a Quaker family enterprise with a sense of community deeply ingrained through every bit of its DNA ... It led the way in terms of employee welfare. It paid high wages, introduced days off, provided vitamins and free healthcare as well as pensions and unemployment benefits. It even created 'Cadbury villages' where workers, their families and the local community all benefited from improved living conditions.[7]

He concludes:

> The last point I'd make for other companies considering becoming a B Corporation is that I don't think it's a choice between 'doing good' or 'making money'. Purpose driven companies, which understand what it means to make the world a better place, will deliver enormous financial returns for their investors over the coming decades. The Cadbury brothers, Ben and Jerry would all back me up.

Many companies are aware they need to regain the trust of their consumers and communities. Future university–industry alliances are likely to be focused on social innovation. They will be highly innovative in the way they involve interdisciplinary and transdisciplinary research, teaching and KE. They will engage staff and students widely across their institutions to find solutions to the world's most pressing issues. 5th generation universities will use all of the core activities within their mission to find solutions to complex challenges. They will offer partners a triple bottom line return on their investment in a way that is measurable, with objectives and key results.

In the new era post-pandemic, we will see student projects with industry partners integrated with KE. Through work-focused degree programmes and teaching methodologies, industry partners are invited to become technical mentors and join students in the classroom. They can impart their industry-relevant skills and knowledge from practical experience in the real world, as well as offer innovative student projects, work placements and internships. It is far better to have industry partners actively involved than just sitting on an industry advisory board that meets once or twice a year. Deeper engagement with industry helps grow a strong, trusted alliance and delivers the most value to both industry and academia. Growing such partnerships may also attract new students from a more diverse range of backgrounds who may not have thought of the university-route previously. Students will start their working life more industry-ready than ever before but also with a mindset geared to making an impact for societal good in the world. In recent years, some universities are starting to collaborate through arranging teams of students to tackle both vital clinical and also industry projects as part of their academic progression. This is a very positive development.

Craving recognition?

Many universities have similar objectives linked to the pillars of research, education and innovation (also known as KE). For example, they aim to maintain research of the highest quality, impact and profile. Within the UK, where publicly funded universities dominate, there is pressure for universities to be recognised externally in government assessment systems such as the Research Excellence Framework (REF), the Teaching Excellence Framework (TEF) and the Knowledge Exchange Framework (KEF). Universities also aspire to be recognised by industry as valuable partners, and increasingly vice versa.

Universities in the Global South have much to offer, and Global North universities must respect and appreciate this. 5th generation universities will collaborate on multidisciplinary and equitable boundary-spanning research with the Global South to address the UN SDGs. They will be more porous to the outside world, starting with their local communities and moving outwards in scale. They will collaborate with universities that are in very different R&D contexts globally through an alliance of equals rather than an imperialistic approach. Governments and philanthropic foundations have an important role to enable and foster the growth of such transdisciplinary quadruple and quintuple helix interactions between the Global North and Global South for worldwide societal benefit. The growth of such alliance activity may be accelerated today more easily than ever before through new digital collaboration platforms.

Technology transfer

5th generation universities will embrace models of technology transfer based on open and shared IP among universities to tackle societal challenges. It is encouraging that since 2020, Stanford University, Harvard University and Massachusetts Institute of Technology have signed up to the COVID-19 Technology Access Framework, and others united behind a similar model to accelerate development of healthcare solutions during the pandemic. They softened their approach to IP commercialisation and fast-tracked applied research via royalty-free, non-exclusive licences.[8] Similarly, in the UK in 2020, UCL's Institute of Healthcare Engineering released full design and manufacturing instructions, on a zero-cost licence, for the local production of UCL-Ventura CPAP ventilators around the world.[9] 5th generation universities will realise the benefits of partnering at pace to build alliances focused on equitable access and inclusion.

Green jobs and post-pandemic recovery addressing climate action

How has the pandemic changed the political and economic environment for university–industry collaborations? Experts within universities have frequently been in the public gaze over the last two years and the impact of universities has gained greater societal, industrial and government recognition. Businesses face pressure to recover and become more efficient and productive. Following COP26, many are also required and committed to work towards a zero-carbon economy.

Governments around the world want to become leaders in the zero-carbon future, through the creation of many new 'green jobs', for example in renewable energy and vertical farming. The UK government want to create two million of these by 2030, rising from 410,000 in 2021.[10] This will require industry to innovate and for that, leading companies increasingly realise that they need to collaborate with research-intensive universities to reduce risk and uncertainty and leverage government funding as well as to access talent and complementary expertise. As mentioned earlier, over the last decade there has been a huge growth in interest from corporate innovation labs towards addressing sustainability challenges, with significant increase in venture capital directed at 'impact investing'. Green jobs will also require universities to help students develop a new set of both soft and hard skills. Universities must take this task seriously.

What is the role for government in driving forward partnerships to address the climate emergency and set a direction for solving pressing social and environmental problems? Governments should increasingly seek to institutionalise transdisciplinary, multi-sector collaboration in tackling technological, societal and environmental challenges which may not be driven by immediate commercial interest but longer-term value creation for the benefit of society. This could include planning to avoid future pandemics and sensible regulatory reform and streamlining. They should act as a facilitator to enable greater exchange of knowledge through in-person roundtable events and new digital communication channels that will bring together leaders on a transformational mission for positive change. We need a new generation of leaders within academia, industry and government who have a broader perspective, recognising how a return on investment involves patient capital and perseverance.

The National Science Foundation (NSF) in the US are increasingly focused on initiatives that can develop large-scale, transformational, foundational research connected to societal benefit.[11] They realise that meaningful research (whether basic, curiosity driven or use inspired) is connected to societal impact, and many current problems faced by society require multidisciplinary working within academia. They also see the need for greater transdisciplinary working between government, academia, industry, and philanthropic foundations. They set up the Global Research Council (GRC) in 2016,[12] teaming up with government research funding agencies and government leaders around the world to tackle complex 'Global Grand Challenge' problems by unleashing talent at greater speed and scale than ever before to realise social and economic benefits.

COVID-19 has indeed demonstrated the importance of global collaborations across sectors. Global challenges require global talent pools and expertise to find solutions, and the GRC is an exciting step towards recognising the importance of alliances based around shared values, ambitions and mutual trust, for positive change. In addition, the NSF Convergence Accelerator launched in 2019 is an innovative programme that funds multi-sector teams to solve societal challenges (see the case study at the end of this chapter).

Responsible innovation

With increased recognition of the importance of universities for economic development, post-pandemic, comes greater pressure from government for university–industry collaboration to tackle social problems and deliver 'responsible innovation'. According to the UK's main research funding body, UK Research and Innovation (UKRI), responsible innovation is 'a process that takes wider impacts of research and innovation into account ... a collective responsibility where funders, researchers, interested and affected parties, including the public, all have an important role to play'.[13]

Responsible innovation requires leaders in universities, not just senior management, but leaders of different external engagement activities, to recognise our global interdependence, consider what sort of problems need to be solved and what future we wish to work towards. We believe that the UN SDGs are a great summary of the types of problems that humanity needs to solve. For example, challenges such as good health and wellbeing (SDG 3), gender equality (SDG 5), climate action (SDG 13), peace, justice, and strong institutions (SDG 16) all have important ethical considerations for innovation (see Figure 1.13).

Responsible innovation requires a process that is more inclusive and sustainable and involves all innovators, whether researchers, teachers or KE practitioners, to effectively engage with industry, government and the public. A good example here is the booming field of Artificial Intelligence (AI), which has great potential to benefit humanity, but also, however, for harm if we are not careful. Government and academia have an important role to work with civil society and industry to ensure that such technology is harnessed for the common good of humanity.

Alliances between universities, industry and civil society, including the not-for-profit sector are vital for supporting high-quality, relevant teaching and research. Improved collaboration with clinical regulators and standards bodies could also accelerate technologies aimed at achieving the UN SDGs (particularly SDG 3). Industry partners can provide real-world case studies that ground theory and bring alive course content and curriculum, providing engaging stories and learning for students about responsible innovation. Co-creation of content should be encouraged in many subject areas. There is a great opportunity for industry to work with academia to upskill students in their new technologies. This investment makes business sense as students may eventually become users of cloud infrastructure, for example.

Civil society grants legitimacy to societal value creation and helps define 'public value' – value created collectively for a public purpose. This requires citizen or community engagement. To define the 17 UN SDGs, there was widespread consultation among civil society globally to find the challenges that really matter to people everywhere. Universities are ideally placed to work closely with civil society to tackle the UN SDGs locally, nationally, and internationally and to demonstrate impact, relevance, and public value beyond the academy.

Glocalisation

Climate change is a global and local (glocal) emergency. The process of glocalisation is merging the civic role of universities with their increasingly global concerns, as their work towards addressing global challenges is channelled to locally based interventions. Examples include:

- on-campus drives to reduce plastic waste and their institution's carbon footprint;
- improving access for women into higher education (particularly in subjects such as Computer Science that have very low representation of women);
- teaching that fosters a sense of global citizenship;
- citizen-science research aimed at tackling water pollution in local rivers.

The list is endless and will depend on your institution's own context, strengths and interests. What is important is that each university considers how particular global challenges can start to be addressed within their own local environment.

Increasingly, local government (cities or county-devolved administrations) will seek to form more structured partnerships with universities both from within their regions and globally, as working together in a cohort with organisations facing similar challenges, will yield significant benefits.

Do all innovation pathways lead to Silicon Valley?

In this section, we engage with the scholarly literature to discuss innovation theory, systems, processes and environments for R&D, knowledge economies, regional economic development, research 'impact' and how to define 'success'. We will review relevant contributions related to transformational alliances and the UN SDGs. Mariana Mazzucato's latest book *Mission Economy: A Moonshot Guide to Changing Capitalism* (2021)[14] is also highly relevant to our argument and the author also aligns with the arguments of Professor Dan Breznitz in *Innovation in Real Places: Strategies for Prosperity in an Unforgiving World* (2021).[15]

Over the last 20 years, university–industry partnerships have been growing around the world, driven by accelerating technological progress in research-intensive areas such as biotechnology and AI. Digital transformation, including new collaboration tools like Zoom, can help reduce the barriers for setting up new partnerships, particularly with the Global South, creating the potential for many new and exciting global collaborations. This trend looks set to continue post-pandemic, driven by a growing awareness that the complex challenges and social needs the world faces require a concerted collaborative effort involving both public and private sectors. The move towards a zero-carbon economy will arguably require greater interdisciplinary knowledge-sharing and innovation than ever before.

Breznitz argues that not all universities in the world should follow the dominant Silicon Valley model of innovation to deliver growth in their regions. He believes that the innovation policies of countries and regions should not be wedded to 'novelty innovation' driven by venture capital and globally competitive universities as 'the world has changed and there are many, many different paths to innovation-based growth'.[16] He defines innovation as 'any activity along the process of taking new ideas and devising new or improved products and services and putting them in the market'. He suggests that innovation follows four stages, each of which can happen at different places around the world today:

1. Novelty (the Silicon Valley model)
2. Design, prototype development, and production engineering
3. Second-generation product and component innovation (Germany is focusing on this area)
4. Production and assembly

Breznitz rightly highlights the globalisation of the innovation process and the importance of diverse models. Creativity and invention are one part of the process, but innovation requires application to real-world problems. We believe a fifth stage of innovation could be described as 'multi-sector mobilisation for societal benefit' focused on finding new commercialisation pathways to deploy innovation to the people who most need it. For example, there is the huge challenge of vaccinating the billions of people around the world against coronavirus. 5th generation universities will have a key underpinning and influencing role in embedding and delivering this fifth stage of innovation, working together with charities, governments and industry across the quadruple helix while delivering positive change to the environment through the quintuple helix (see Figure 1.2). Will society, though, be ready for this?

How can your university work with industries that span continents? Industry has a mutual interest in designing the products and services of the future, as well as talent. Wherever there are shared values, mutual trust and aspirations for positive change, great things are possible when working together. There is no need to compromise transparency or research integrity.

5th generation universities will identify and map out the problem areas where they have relevant expertise and capability and can collaborate in a transdisciplinary way. These universities will have the motivation and tools to synergise collective efforts. They will create a sense of urgency within their institutions to tackle large societal problems that their research community care about, to deliver positive change. They proactively share their value propositions with potential partners to unleash exciting new projects in their regions and beyond, seeking to accelerate and scale up activity for positive societal change. Governments will be eager to support such ambitious universities by catalysing and enabling such efforts through mission-led funding that will bring together collective interests for public good. They will encourage a convergence of co-investment from industry and philanthropy.

In his book, Breznitz is critical of the conventional wisdom that the Silicon Valley model of innovation is what all universities should be aiming for.[17] Is gentrification and unbridled capitalism, particularly in Western democracies, leading to inequality? There is no doubt that Cambridge and Oxford's technology clusters have created many high-tech jobs for their regions as well as lower-paid roles. However, rising property prices caused by the success of Silicon Valley and Oxbridge have priced many local residents out of the market.

Breznitz argues that people do not consider the potential impact of following the path of the Silicon Valley model. He suggests that Taiwan, Sweden and Finland are places that have excelled in an innovation model specialising in the last three stages of innovation (in our earlier list). However, in our view, it is imperative not to negate the importance of states seeking to develop globally competitive universities that seek to make a high impact in the world by solving global challenges. For example, Oxford University produced the first widespread affordable COVID-19 vaccine through an alliance with AstraZeneca.

What would the innovation arising from a 5th generation university look like in your region? In future, they will create systems and mechanisms of corporate engagement activities that have a good fit to the socioeconomic conditions and innovation ecosystems of their localities. Universities need to understand the unique selling point (USP) of their location to address the most relevant SDGs for their context as well as more widely. They need to know what the availability of talent is within their region, and what financial resource is necessary to guarantee and sustain impact.

5th generation university innovation tactics will take account of local, regional, national and international context as they position their institutions within the global marketplace. Alliances are vital for enabling a robust and effective innovation ecosystem in any region. Mechanisms to enable alliances geared towards innovation can include science and business parks close to universities and 'Living Labs'. These are public–private testbeds that offer transformative research, education and innovation opportunities for students, staff and graduates, as well as local school children. Government research funding agencies have an important role to facilitate and support such mechanisms that can help accelerate research into practice and solutions for the benefit of society.

Such Living Labs are not limited to science and technology disciplines. Cardiff University in Wales set up a Social Science Research Park[18] encompassing a large area of lettable units, including wet labs and co-working space designed to increase the successful translation of research and innovation processes into new and improved commercial products, processes and services. The Park includes co-location of all the university's major social science research centres and institutes alongside research collaborators from the private, public and third sectors. They are all working together with the aim of addressing major societal challenges.

Challenge-oriented and commercially aware strategy

5th generation universities are challenge oriented. How can you set and implement a credible strategy that is not just SDG-oriented and commercially aware, but also aligns with your institutional mission? Universities like Canterbury Christ Church University want to: work in partnership with our students to ensure they graduate with an understanding of the challenges facing society and our world, and have the skills, commitment and personal qualities needed to address them.[19]

Being more commercially aware will help 5th generation universities achieve positive change at greater pace, leveraging their assets to create new industries and grow entrepreneurial talent. By focusing on socially aware innovation, they will generate the economic growth needed to help lift people out of poverty. A commercially aware strategy recognises the potential of entrepreneurship accelerators, for example to leverage the creativity of student and staff entrepreneurs.

Embedding corporate engagement within your university strategy

Where does corporate engagement sit within a 5th generation university? We think it is best within a dedicated centralised and well-resourced Strategic Alliance and Corporate Engagement Team reporting to a VP (Research and Innovation). The team will also liaise with individual alliance leads embedded within academic departments. Such a team will have the right skillsets needed (often gained from experience in industry) to manage partnerships for positive change wisely, as good stewards, ensuring that data on industry relationships is shared internally. This will mean that a Technology Transfer Office (TTO) will not handle all transactional IP licensing negotiations with an industry partner distinct from understanding the philanthropic or research links with the same company.

Such an approach as described here requires effective internal communication. The corporate engagement team will have a 360-degree understanding of most of the corporate activity on campus. They will adopt a tiered approach to alliance management to improve coordination and prioritisation of the most valued corporates. This streamlining of external engagement functions helps to avoid multiple touchpoints for industry (see Tables 1.4 and 2.6).

The VP (Research and Innovation) will oversee both industry and philanthropic relations, research and innovation contracts, as well as the activity of the TTO, and develop a shared, non-competitive language of internal and external communications. He/she will encourage strong cooperation between the various external engagement teams within his/her responsibility, whether central, faculty or within departments. This senior leader will adopt a proactive, stewardship attitude and approach to engaging with and maximising value from industry partners. This approach seeks to understand and appreciate current needs as well as anticipate the future needs of allies. For example, partner requirements of corporates have become more complex and varied in recent years, with many seeking Master Research Agreements (MRAs) that combine philanthropic, sponsored research and innovation elements. Research Services teams must be trained to deliver high-quality support from pre-award through to contract and post-award, in partnership with relevant academic departments in a way that helps to support the academic mission effectively.

Alongside the centralised strategic alliance functionality, all industry alliances within 5th generation universities will involve the Dean of the most relevant academic faculty providing executive sponsorship internally as designated by the VP (Research and Innovation). This provides the inertia to carry important alliances forward from the bottom up, and respects the relationships held by academics in departments while broadening these relationships for the benefit of the whole university and wider society.

As an African proverb says, 'it takes a village to raise a child', and senior leadership, led by the Provost and VP (Research and Innovation) must encourage all staff to have an alliance mindset to provide for and interact positively with external organisations. This mindset will enable these relationships to remain healthy and add value. Corporate engagement strategies from senior management need to balance research impact with translational impact towards achieving the UN SDGs. TTOs will prioritise commercialisation and translational impact, while other teams within the VP (Research and Innovation)'s office may highlight the impact of research, teaching or other forms of KE. If your strategy is focused on growing start-ups and spinouts rather than just licensing, finding corporate partners with venturing arms will be important.

The UN's Six Principles for Responsible Management Education

Technology can help facilitate the achievement of UN SDGs. However, technology alone, without the education of business and political leaders combined with civil society support, will not be a significant driver of transformational change. This is why the UN's Six Principles for Responsible Management Education (PRME) initiative is so important.[20] It aims to foster a new generation of business leaders who understand the importance of sustainability and partnership. Table 2.3 highlights these Six Principles.

5th generation universities will consider how such principles can be implemented among not just business students but all students through a curriculum to bring about culture change. They will highlight the importance of partnerships and alliances. They will also consider how staff leadership and management professional development programmes can incorporate training around building strong internal and external alliances across the different academic and professional services career stages.

Towards a more ethical capitalism? The B Corp Movement and Wellbeing Economies

The B Corp Movement started in 2006 when three friends with business and private equity backgrounds created an organisation 'dedicated to making it easier for mission-driven companies to protect and improve their positive impact over time'.[21] B Corp certification is to business what Fair Trade certification is to coffee. There are now almost 4,000 Certified B Corporations in more than 70 countries covering 150 different industries.

Table 2.3: The UN's Six Principles for Responsible Management Education

UN PRME principle	Description
1 – Purpose	We will develop the capabilities of students to be future generators of sustainable value for business and society at large and to work for an inclusive and sustainable global economy.
2 – Values	We will incorporate into our academic activities, curricula, and organisational practices the values of global social responsibility as portrayed in international initiatives such as the United Nations Global Compact.
3 – Method	We will create educational frameworks, materials, processes and environments that enable effective learning experiences for responsible leadership.
4 – Research	We will engage in conceptual and empirical research that advances our understanding about the role, dynamics and impact of corporations in the creation of sustainable social, environmental and economic value.
5 – Partnership	We will interact with managers of business corporations to extend our knowledge of their challenges in meeting social and environmental responsibilities and to explore jointly effective approaches to meeting these challenges.
6 – Dialogue	We will facilitate and support dialogue and debate among educators, students, business, government, consumers, media, civil society organisations and other interested groups and stakeholders on critical issues related to global social responsibility and sustainability.

Certification is undertaken by a non-profit organisation with a team of analysts who have developed impact management and stakeholder governance tools called 'B Lab'. While the majority are small businesses, there are publicly traded, multinational companies too, such as Ben & Jerry's. The 'B Economy' aims to foster a new global business environment that balances purpose and profit where 'companies are legally required to consider the impact of their decisions on their workers, customers, suppliers, community, and the environment. This is a community of leaders, driving a global movement of people using business as a force for good'.[22]

The growth in Certified B Corporations and the social entrepreneurship movement more generally are encouraging means 'change for the better' and sees improvement as a gradual process that involves all employees in a culture of healthy experimentation and reflection on what works. 5th generation universities will incorporate this into their very DNA.

Higher education institutions have an ethical responsibility to embrace becoming a learning organisation to boost their progress towards achieving their institutional missions. Such universities will share best practice around KE, external engagement and alliance activity internally and with other universities and industry. They maintain a 'lessons learned' as well as a 'benefits realised' record (this could form part of a customer relationship management, or CRM, system) for every alliance that they are involved with. This ensures that mistakes can be avoided for future alliance development, and internal processes can be continually improved and optimised.

Universities will need to acquire the ability to evaluate their success through benchmarking to ensure that they become increasingly effective at strategic alliance building. They have a 'glocal' place-based orientation that understands and maximises benefit from their own physical, regional and national context towards their KE efforts particularly. These universities seek to influence through collaboration, to create shared value, and to bring about positive change and impact in their local and regional innovation ecosystems. As mentioned in Chapter 1, many universities struggle to communicate their uniqueness and value within their localities and regions to prospective partners. 5th generation universities have learned to do this well, including using digital collaboration platforms.

For every partnership that your institution builds, at every level, from individual academic to whole department, school or institution, staff should be encouraged to ask regularly 'what have we learned?' and 'how will this change what I do in future in terms of our research, teaching and innovation?'. They should share their alliance stories and journeys with colleagues and students.

signs that a more ethical and inclusive capitalism valuing higher standards of social and environmental performance, transparency and accountability is being birthed. Many multinational corporations now highlight how their companies are contributing to different UN SDGs on their websites. A new commercial environment is emerging where companies are expected to deliver social purpose and engage a wider range of more critical stakeholders. This goes beyond CSR and is about a reformation in company practices and focus. New Generation Z talent entering industry value the UN SDGs and believe that both economic and social goals matter for good businesses.

The interest in 'Wellbeing Economies' by governments mirrors the business interest in B Corporations. The Wellbeing Economy Alliance (WEAll) is a 10-year project that arose out of several local and global movements coming together focused on a common goal of encouraging a reorientation of the economic system towards 'sustainable wellbeing' in many countries.[23] WEAll helped to initiate a collaboration of national and regional governments currently comprising Scotland, New Zealand, Iceland, Finland and Wales called the Wellbeing Economy Governments (WEGo) in 2018. The partnership promotes innovative, shared policy making for change that advances their shared ambition of building wellbeing economies with a strong focus on making progress towards the UN SDGs, in line with Goal 17.

The First Minister of Scotland, Nicola Sturgeon, gave a TED talk in July 2019 titled 'Why governments should prioritize wellbeing', arguing that 21st-century 'development' must involve delivering human and ecological wellbeing.[24] Her talk challenged the acceptance of gross domestic product (GDP) as the main measure of a country's success, explaining how GDP values short-term economic activity, without consideration of the ecological damage caused by that activity.

WEAll now has over 200 individuals, organisations, governments, academics, communities, and businesses as members although, interestingly, no universities are listed. 5th generation universities will likely become members of such networks as these will play a vital role for transformational collaborative multi-sector efforts that can make a real impact on the transition towards a more sustainable economy.

Measuring impact: the development of impact management systems

Impact is building long-term, trusted, two-way, sustainable relationships that do good and align with your institutional values. Capturing and measuring the impact and societal benefit arising from engagement activity such as forming alliances can be challenging. The UN Global Compact have worked with B Lab to create a web-based impact management solution called 'SDG Action Manager' to enable businesses to operationalise the SDGs during this 'Decade of Action' up to 2030.[25]

Universities can benefit from better impact management to enable them to set goals and track progress related to achieving their institutional missions aligned with wider societal challenges such as the UN SDGs. This should include improved tracking of university–industry alliance activities and how these contribute to achieving their goals. Universities should gain a better understanding of how their supply chains and operations achieve positive impact. Impact management systems should also feature a consideration of risks for different SDGs, for example if tackling UN SDG 5 (gender equality), there would be a risk in partnering with organisations that do not have strong diversity and inclusion values. The urgency for universities to measure impact has been accelerated by government funding instruments such as REF, KEF and TEF in the UK, for example.

In the UK system where research is evaluated by the government's REF review every few years, demonstrating 'impact' has become a vital requirement for all publicly funded universities. This has led to a greater focus on writing high impact case studies as part of a REF submission, and universities often employ specialist copywriters to shape these. Likewise, in university fellowship and grant applications, public funders will include an 'impact statement' to be provided.

Ensuring that academics have an end-user in mind for their research is important; however, unfortunately, demonstrating impact is sometimes seen as a tick-box exercise rather than an important part of the role of an academic and a university more widely. The need to secure letters of support from industry partners can facilitate a utilitarian and transactional mindset

in engaging with industry, rather than a genuine, deep an sustainable collaboration.

Are you able to tell a great story about your university's impact?

Cave paintings dating back millennia have been found all arou the world; however, it is likely that most caves with paintings still waiting to be discovered. Anthropologists, archaeologists theologians tell us that storytelling is central to human exister Creating and recording compelling stories about the impac your alliances is crucial to maintain and grow momentum buy-in from key influencers in both the university and indu These should include examples about the impact of your rese teaching and innovation activities through transformati alliances with others.

What are your 'hooks' in the narrative of your univer approach to alliances that will create interest, urgency an emotional desire to engage among prospective allies? In examples on your website of case studies of how you with industry partners in diverse ways for mutual benefit. Cases' are extremely valuable for both university and in partners but are often neglected by universities because of of marketing resource. They can illustrate student exper as well as the innovation and talent pipeline developmer help to build the brands of both parties. For student p involving industry, it is important to encourage stude produce video/written case studies as part of their asses These can then be used on the university website or you media as marketing collateral.

5th generation universities as 'learning organisations'

Universities can sometimes become known for a blame due to a high level of internal politics between depar faculties and central units. In the not-too-distant universities will become true 'learning organisations'[26] area of their activity, with a continuous improvement approach to their partnerships. *Kaizen* is a Japanese w

Entrepreneurship Readiness Level and incentivisation of staff

Table 2.4 compares the different traits and skills of leaders, managers, entrepreneurs and researchers within a university (based on our own analysis, observations and industry experience). Helping academics to increase their entrepreneurial readiness level (or capacity) (ERL) is an important part of creating an enabling environment for transformational strategic alliances to flourish. This environment is not just dependent on a particular unique type of entrepreneur, rather it depends on having a diverse mix of leaders, entrepreneurs, managers and researchers with an openness to working and understanding industry imperatives (see Table 2.4).

It is useful to consider the diversity of academic profiles in a typical academic department when it comes to industry collaboration. It is striking to note the similar character traits between academics and researchers who are highly effective in forging alliances with industry and entrepreneurs. We have noted that the most highly cited academic papers, for example in AI, are often those written in partnership with leading corporates. These academics are more likely to have patents and to have created start-ups. However, current incentivisation structures in universities may not encourage academics to pursue industry engagement and undertake KE activity more broadly. University leaders should consider how the environment for alliances can be

Table 2.4: Comparing and contrasting the typical characteristics of leaders, managers, entrepreneurs and researchers

Leaders	Managers	Entrepreneurs	Researchers
Charisma	Analysis	Calculated risk	Scholastic
Foresight	Delivery focus	Visionary	Visionary
Empowering	Operational	Innovative	Innovative
Compassionate	Appreciative	Socially aware	Ethically aware
Servant-hearted	Systematic	Ambitious	Ambitious
Humble	Target-orientated	Purposeful	Focused
Adaptable	Agile	Commercially skilful	Commercially aware

improved through incentivisation structures that will help raise their ERL and grow role models among their staff.

Many people think that leaders and managers are the same, but they require very different skills and character traits to succeed. 5th generation universities will need leaders and managers who collaborate effectively through distributed teams in departments, faculties and central units pursuing innovative external engagement in a highly coordinated and unified way to achieve the university's common goals. Such leaders have no reservations about collaboration, they are wise, servant-hearted, humble, empowering to their staff and open and adaptable to learn. The best managers are also generally good leaders, in our experience. They are highly focused on delivering objectives and are results orientated. We consider management and leadership of alliances further in Chapters 3 and 4.

Entrepreneurial universities require entrepreneurial academics. In the current social environment where levels of uncertainty are very high, due to rapid social change, having an entrepreneurial mindset among researchers wishing to deliver impact and create change will become increasingly important. 5th generation universities will assess the ERL of their institution.

5th generation universities with a high ERL level will also provide unparalleled opportunities for students to learn entrepreneurship skills within innovation lab environments and to set up their own companies. Students will increasingly form start-ups with their academic supervisors, and they will begin an entrepreneurial learning journey together.

Centres for Doctoral Training (CDTs) are a successful UKRI initiative for delivering thematic and cohort-based PhD centres. A significant number of their doctoral students are part- or fully funded by industry, and students can gain work experience as part of their career development. CDTs can be a powerhouse of student entrepreneurship, new approaches to pedagogy, innovation and corporate engagement, helping to increase the ERL of your institution as PhD students transition to become postdocs and academics where they will grow the entrepreneurial culture through transformational strategic alliances with industry.

signs that a more ethical and inclusive capitalism valuing higher standards of social and environmental performance, transparency and accountability is being birthed. Many multinational corporations now highlight how their companies are contributing to different UN SDGs on their websites. A new commercial environment is emerging where companies are expected to deliver social purpose and engage a wider range of more critical stakeholders. This goes beyond CSR and is about a reformation in company practices and focus. New Generation Z talent entering industry value the UN SDGs and believe that both economic and social goals matter for good businesses.

The interest in 'Wellbeing Economies' by governments mirrors the business interest in B Corporations. The Wellbeing Economy Alliance (WEAll) is a 10-year project that arose out of several local and global movements coming together focused on a common goal of encouraging a reorientation of the economic system towards 'sustainable wellbeing' in many countries.[23] WEAll helped to initiate a collaboration of national and regional governments currently comprising Scotland, New Zealand, Iceland, Finland and Wales called the Wellbeing Economy Governments (WEGo) in 2018. The partnership promotes innovative, shared policy making for change that advances their shared ambition of building wellbeing economies with a strong focus on making progress towards the UN SDGs, in line with Goal 17.

The First Minister of Scotland, Nicola Sturgeon, gave a TED talk in July 2019 titled 'Why governments should prioritize wellbeing', arguing that 21st-century 'development' must involve delivering human and ecological wellbeing.[24] Her talk challenged the acceptance of gross domestic product (GDP) as the main measure of a country's success, explaining how GDP values short-term economic activity, without consideration of the ecological damage caused by that activity.

WEAll now has over 200 individuals, organisations, governments, academics, communities, and businesses as members although, interestingly, no universities are listed. 5th generation universities will likely become members of such networks as these will play a vital role for transformational collaborative multi-sector efforts that can make a real impact on the transition towards a more sustainable economy.

Measuring impact: the development of impact management systems

Impact is building long-term, trusted, two-way, sustainable relationships that do good and align with your institutional values. Capturing and measuring the impact and societal benefit arising from engagement activity such as forming alliances can be challenging. The UN Global Compact have worked with B Lab to create a web-based impact management solution called 'SDG Action Manager' to enable businesses to operationalise the SDGs during this 'Decade of Action' up to 2030.[25]

Universities can benefit from better impact management to enable them to set goals and track progress related to achieving their institutional missions aligned with wider societal challenges such as the UN SDGs. This should include improved tracking of university–industry alliance activities and how these contribute to achieving their goals. Universities should gain a better understanding of how their supply chains and operations achieve positive impact. Impact management systems should also feature a consideration of risks for different SDGs, for example if tackling UN SDG 5 (gender equality), there would be a risk in partnering with organisations that do not have strong diversity and inclusion values. The urgency for universities to measure impact has been accelerated by government funding instruments such as REF, KEF and TEF in the UK, for example.

In the UK system where research is evaluated by the government's REF review every few years, demonstrating 'impact' has become a vital requirement for all publicly funded universities. This has led to a greater focus on writing high impact case studies as part of a REF submission, and universities often employ specialist copywriters to shape these. Likewise, in university fellowship and grant applications, public funders will include an 'impact statement' to be provided.

Ensuring that academics have an end-user in mind for their research is important; however, unfortunately, demonstrating impact is sometimes seen as a tick-box exercise rather than an important part of the role of an academic and a university more widely. The need to secure letters of support from industry partners can facilitate a utilitarian and transactional mindset in engaging with industry, rather than a genuine, deep and sustainable collaboration.

Are you able to tell a great story about your university's impact?

Cave paintings dating back millennia have been found all around the world; however, it is likely that most caves with paintings are still waiting to be discovered. Anthropologists, archaeologists and theologians tell us that storytelling is central to human existence. Creating and recording compelling stories about the impact of your alliances is crucial to maintain and grow momentum and buy-in from key influencers in both the university and industry. These should include examples about the impact of your research, teaching and innovation activities through transformational alliances with others.

What are your 'hooks' in the narrative of your university's approach to alliances that will create interest, urgency and an emotional desire to engage among prospective allies? Include examples on your website of case studies of how you work with industry partners in diverse ways for mutual benefit. 'Use Cases' are extremely valuable for both university and industry partners but are often neglected by universities because of a lack of marketing resource. They can illustrate student experience as well as the innovation and talent pipeline development that help to build the brands of both parties. For student projects involving industry, it is important to encourage students to produce video/written case studies as part of their assessment. These can then be used on the university website or your social media as marketing collateral.

5th generation universities as 'learning organisations'

Universities can sometimes become known for a blame culture due to a high level of internal politics between departments, faculties and central units. In the not-too-distant future, universities will become true 'learning organisations'[26] in every area of their activity, with a continuous improvement 'kaizen' approach to their partnerships. Kaizen is a Japanese word that means 'change for the better' and sees improvement as a gradual process that involves all employees in a culture of healthy experimentation and reflection on what works. 5th generation universities will incorporate this into their very DNA.

Higher education institutions have an ethical responsibility to embrace becoming a learning organisation to boost their progress towards achieving their institutional missions. Such universities will share best practice around KE, external engagement and alliance activity internally and with other universities and industry. They maintain a 'lessons learned' as well as a 'benefits realised' record (this could form part of a customer relationship management, or CRM, system) for every alliance that they are involved with. This ensures that mistakes can be avoided for future alliance development, and internal processes can be continually improved and optimised.

Universities will need to acquire the ability to evaluate their success through benchmarking to ensure that they become increasingly effective at strategic alliance building. They have a 'glocal' place-based orientation that understands and maximises benefit from their own physical, regional and national context towards their KE efforts particularly. These universities seek to influence through collaboration, to create shared value, and to bring about positive change and impact in their local and regional innovation ecosystems. As mentioned in Chapter 1, many universities struggle to communicate their uniqueness and value within their localities and regions to prospective partners. 5th generation universities have learned to do this well, including using digital collaboration platforms.

For every partnership that your institution builds, at every level, from individual academic to whole department, school or institution, staff should be encouraged to ask regularly 'what have we learned?' and 'how will this change what I do in future in terms of our research, teaching and innovation?'. They should share their alliance stories and journeys with colleagues and students.

Entrepreneurship Readiness Level and incentivisation of staff

Table 2.4 compares the different traits and skills of leaders, managers, entrepreneurs and researchers within a university (based on our own analysis, observations and industry experience). Helping academics to increase their entrepreneurial readiness level (or capacity) (ERL) is an important part of creating an enabling environment for transformational strategic alliances to flourish. This environment is not just dependent on a particular unique type of entrepreneur, rather it depends on having a diverse mix of leaders, entrepreneurs, managers and researchers with an openness to working and understanding industry imperatives (see Table 2.4).

It is useful to consider the diversity of academic profiles in a typical academic department when it comes to industry collaboration. It is striking to note the similar character traits between academics and researchers who are highly effective in forging alliances with industry and entrepreneurs. We have noted that the most highly cited academic papers, for example in AI, are often those written in partnership with leading corporates. These academics are more likely to have patents and to have created start-ups. However, current incentivisation structures in universities may not encourage academics to pursue industry engagement and undertake KE activity more broadly. University leaders should consider how the environment for alliances can be

Table 2.4: Comparing and contrasting the typical characteristics of leaders, managers, entrepreneurs and researchers

Leaders	Managers	Entrepreneurs	Researchers
Charisma	Analysis	Calculated risk	Scholastic
Foresight	Delivery focus	Visionary	Visionary
Empowering	Operational	Innovative	Innovative
Compassionate	Appreciative	Socially aware	Ethically aware
Servant-hearted	Systematic	Ambitious	Ambitious
Humble	Target-orientated	Purposeful	Focused
Adaptable	Agile	Commercially skilful	Commercially aware

improved through incentivisation structures that will help raise their ERL and grow role models among their staff.

Many people think that leaders and managers are the same, but they require very different skills and character traits to succeed. 5th generation universities will need leaders and managers who collaborate effectively through distributed teams in departments, faculties and central units pursuing innovative external engagement in a highly coordinated and unified way to achieve the university's common goals. Such leaders have no reservations about collaboration, they are wise, servant-hearted, humble, empowering to their staff and open and adaptable to learn. The best managers are also generally good leaders, in our experience. They are highly focused on delivering objectives and are results orientated. We consider management and leadership of alliances further in Chapters 3 and 4.

Entrepreneurial universities require entrepreneurial academics. In the current social environment where levels of uncertainty are very high, due to rapid social change, having an entrepreneurial mindset among researchers wishing to deliver impact and create change will become increasingly important. 5th generation universities will assess the ERL of their institution.

5th generation universities with a high ERL level will also provide unparalleled opportunities for students to learn entrepreneurship skills within innovation lab environments and to set up their own companies. Students will increasingly form start-ups with their academic supervisors, and they will begin an entrepreneurial learning journey together.

Centres for Doctoral Training (CDTs) are a successful UKRI initiative for delivering thematic and cohort-based PhD centres. A significant number of their doctoral students are part- or fully funded by industry, and students can gain work experience as part of their career development. CDTs can be a powerhouse of student entrepreneurship, new approaches to pedagogy, innovation and corporate engagement, helping to increase the ERL of your institution as PhD students transition to become postdocs and academics where they will grow the entrepreneurial culture through transformational strategic alliances with industry.

Understanding cultural differences between sectors

When considering transformational strategic alliances, it is important to understand the significant differences in culture and values between universities and industry (Table 2.5). An improved

Table 2.5: Finding complementarity between the diverse cultures of industry and universities

Industry	University	Complementarity – how to achieve alignment
Product focused and market driven	Publication driven	Brand and reputational benefits
Wealth creation	Knowledge creation	Knowledge exchange and co-production, co-publication, technology/talent pipelines and innovation ecosystem among staff and students
Fast paced	Slower paced	Commitment or delivery plan with regular communication around deadlines and featuring go/no-go gates
Agile	Many competing priorities	Projects of strong mutual interest to solve research problems affecting whole fields/industry sectors
Shareholder value	Public good	Co-value creation for mutual and societal benefit (triple win)
Commercially focused and technology agnostic	Enthusiastic about technology but not always clear or realistic about benefits	Low-cost, low-risk student project to explore ideas, develop proof of concept demonstrators and grow trust
Proprietary innovation focus	Open source preferable	Flexibility around collaborative models with costings for different IP options
Applied and results driven research; higher Technology Readiness Level (TRL)	Mainly curiosity-driven, fundamental research; low TRL	Interest in expanding perspectives and understanding of the underlying science
Objectives aligning to overall business strategy	Academic freedom	Address together UN SDGs that pose an existential threat to humanity

understanding of drivers for different sectors can help to avoid culture clashes, for example the pace and agility of the corporate world is considerably greater than that of academia. Therefore, to find an alignment between both cultures, the use of clear commitment or delivery plans featuring deadlines, project stages and 'go/no-go' gates where extra funding may be released dependent on progress, is an important tool for strategic alliance success.

It is generally beneficial to distil challenges facing industry into research problems that need to be solved if you wish to gain the interest and engagement of academics. Industry needs to recognise that not every collaboration with academia will lead to a product; however, it will result in new knowledge that will provide a wider perspective on a problem statement and organisational learning. There will also likely be indirect benefits such as boosting your company's talent pipeline because of engagement through student projects sponsored by industry.

As you can see, divergent organisational cultures exist and must be managed carefully through effective structures of engagement and through the involvement of individuals with the right skillsets, experience and motivation. Universities do indeed need to become more entrepreneurial; however, the term 'entrepreneurial' is not as attractive to some academics as 'mission-focused' – a term that aligns better with the academic mission of universities.

Agility and resilience in academia

Is your university a lion or a gazelle? The strategy of the 5th generation university needs to be emergent and agile, able to adjust rapidly to a world with a seemingly exponential rate of change. Universities that are more agile can make a significant contribution to grand challenges and ensure that significant real-world impact is achieved. An agile working culture can improve efficiency using collaboration technologies that avoid unnecessarily long emails and face-to-face meetings. Collaboration on writing documents concurrently among a team can save significant time emailing documents back and forth with tracked changes.

The pandemic has accelerated change which has driven universities to become more agile than ever before in response to the need to deliver digital education ranging from distance learning to teleworking. This continues to demand innovation in the business models and operational management of universities to create positive change, maintain resilience and ensure continuing academic excellence and progress towards institutional goals. 5th generation university leaders will develop an agile mindset and promote agility across their operations, including within their partnership activities. They will learn from agile software development methodology that focuses on the need for cross-functional teams implementing business agility in their organisational structure and operations to succeed in an uncertain, changing environment.

The importance of in-kind and non-cash contributions from industry

Universities need to move away from instrumentalist and utilitarian understandings of 'impact' and consider non-monetary-value measurements that take account of ROI more broadly. This would include improved recording and accounting of 'in-kind' contributions such as the time of industry mentors, equipment donations, and access to valuable data and connections that cannot otherwise be obtained. This is very important as the value that companies bring to universities cannot just be measured in cash alone.

Valuations of in-kind contributions cannot be disconnected from the valuation that companies do themselves, for example before they write a letter of support for a new research grant proposal that an academic may suggest. 5th generation universities incorporate data on in-kind contributions from their alliance partners into CRM systems so they can have a more accurate record of the benefit that has come from their corporate engagement activity. The UK's PETRAS National Internet of Things Research Hub project involving a number of research-intensive universities and over 100 industry partners is a leading example of how to effectively capture both in-kind and cash contributions in large-scale multi-party projects.[27]

Purposeful partnerships

How do the practices and rhythms that make up the common life of universities convey and uphold the university's ethos and values, such as embodied within their institutional mission statements? How do universities benefit not only individual students, but also their local communities? The SDGs presume an ethical obligation to act against poverty and injustice. Academic and author Albert Cheng wisely asks: 'Is education too focused on information over formation? Is this a recipe for malformation?'[28]

The University of Worcester in the UK has a strong focus on vocational education, training teachers and nurses, and provides an interesting case study. Their courses promote ethical and responsible behaviour, encouraging an understanding of the values of sustainability, inclusion and mutual respect. Their website asserts the importance of 'purposeful partnerships with schools, hospitals, health trusts and others' and highlights that they have a "constantly reinvigorated strategy for purposeful partnerships."[29] The University gives students and graduates the chance to be involved in this work as a key engine for opportunity, creativity, wealth creation and improved public services for their region and beyond.

As mentioned, and as shown in Table 2.1, leaders of 5th generation universities will have a crystal-clear vision and plan (VSEM) for enhancing external engagement with corporates, as successful alliances involve the need for compatibility, cooperation and alignment between individuals, the proposed alliance objectives and each organisation. Individuals need to be personally motivated and interested in contributing to make alliances a success, as they will often need to overcome internal barriers to succeed. In short, they need to be driven by a strong purpose.

Why should industry innovate? Not just to remain competitive and deliver new products and services to meet consumer demand, but increasingly also to address challenges affecting humanity. We are all interdependent, and so this makes long-term business sense. Corporate Venture Capital (CVC) and funds from corporate foundations can be used to achieve great good for humanity when directed at achieving impact linked to the UN SDGs.

Compassionate university community

If your university is marinated by compassionate leadership seeking to implement mission-driven research, education and innovation, a more compassionate, externally, UN SDG-focused university culture can emerge. Such an environment provides the soil in which transformational strategic alliances can grow between Global North and Global South universities and industry around the world. What constitutes a 'compassionate university'? In her book *Towards the Compassionate University: From Golden Thread to Global Impact*, academic Kathryn Waddington lists several factors, and illustrates that compassion is a 'process'.[30]

Innovation districts and ecosystems

5th generation universities will harness new transdisciplinary campus developments to grow 'innovation districts' so they can attract leading corporates to collaborate and form strategic alliances that will bring positive change to their local urban or rural area. They will leverage through these alliances the resources of corporate venture capital and strategic corporate philanthropy once a trusted relationship has been established.

In the UK, several British universities are calling for new policies to expand research districts and foster innovation. Alice Gast, President of Imperial College London, said in an opinion piece in the *Financial Times*: 'The moment has come for co-ordinated policies to expand innovation districts around universities in places such as Glasgow, Manchester, Cambridge and London.'[31]

A key focus area and responsibility for effective alliances within innovation districts and ecosystems should be promoting and maintaining a culture of inclusiveness and diversity of talent. This will require mutually agreed targets and roadmaps involving different sector 'champions' from industry, academia, local government, civil society and philanthropic foundations, targeting their resources towards SDGs such as:

- SDG 4 – Quality education

- SDG 5 – Gender equality
- SDG 8 – Decent work and economic growth
- SDG 10 – Reduced inequalities
- SDG 11 – Sustainable cities and communities

Student demand for work-based learning and upskilling

Educators face the challenges of navigating digital transformation, adapting to new ways of teaching and collaboration online. EdTech is now a rapidly growing market. Technology providers like Microsoft are growing tools like LinkedIn Learning that offers accreditation directly onto members' LinkedIn profiles.

For students' career development, alongside gaining a degree, industry experience and connections throughout university are more important than ever. How are universities facilitating this demand from students for more personalised learning journeys that increase employability? The best approaches involve co-creation with students in their learning journey that empowers them to take hold of new opportunities to undertake work placements within industry and gain entrepreneurial experience. This includes learning about both for-profit and social enterprise business models. Innovative teaching formats include utilising scenario-based learning from real-world examples, taught by a combination of academic staff and guests from industry. Students are increasingly motivated to contribute towards addressing grand societal challenges and this will require diversifying and scaling teaching and learning through multi-sector alliances focused on more inclusive access to global education.

Student projects with industry offer a triple win – for universities, their students and their industry partners. They are a low-cost, low-risk and high-return way for companies and universities to collaborate and they can be the first step to a transformational strategic alliance by providing a place where universities and industry can test, sometimes make mistakes, learn from their engagement, and grow networks of trust. Companies benefit from growing their 'talent pipeline', by finding students that they can recruit on graduating who are 'industry ready', and universities gain from students improving their employability and learning real-world insights about industry. Often students return from experiences of industry internships with greater motivation for their academic work. Risk management is important for both academia and industry in collaborations. As trust builds, risks start to decrease for both parties as the collaboration develops. Developing ideas into solutions that are far from market poses the highest risk for companies but a far lower risk for universities.

Companies that set up joint Centres of Excellence with universities can really benefit from boosting their talent pipeline and gaining greater brand recognition on campus among talented students and staff. Universities who already have the structures and tools in place in their curriculum to offer work-based learning in partnership with industry (either remote, blended or on-premises), will be at a great advantage, by helping to create graduates who are 'industry ready'.

Students are learning about the commercial value of implementing new technologies through projects with industry. They are increasingly skilled at networking through social media platforms and showcasing their own projects and ventures through YouTube, GitHub, and crowdfunding platforms.

Significant redundancies resulting from the economic damage caused by the pandemic are leading to a growing demand for upskilling. How will universities adjust and adapt their offerings to meet this changing demand? How can forming alliances with, for example, global technology providers help as the world also sees new technologies like AI and blockchain replace certain jobs and create new opportunities? 5th generation universities will be focused on offering short courses with certification that provide training in the necessary digital skills and the soft skills such as creativity, leadership and teamworking that will remain vital for future job opportunities.

Partnerships beyond the STEM disciplines

Are university–industry collaborations only relevant for activities in STEM disciplines (Science, Technology, Engineering and Maths)? The arts and humanities have a vital role in maximising impact towards achieving the SDGs, highlighting social justice issues, for example, and how peaceful, more inclusive societies can develop.

This is only possible through forming transformational alliances with multi-sector partners; however, academics within the arts and humanities particularly often worry about whether academic freedom is threatened by working with companies. The response to these concerns is better communication with industry from the outset, and a willingness to learn from a diverse range of people in different sectors who see problems from a diversity of perspectives.

5th generation universities will encourage all staff across disciplinary boundaries to collaborate on addressing challenges that require a multifaceted set of skills and expertise. They will engage with industry to address the UN SDGs through greater use of technologies such as AI and machine learning (ML), where understandings of the ethical, political and philosophical issues in using such technologies responsibly are vital.

The right people with the right skills

Good KE staff are an incredible asset providing you with transformational collaborative advantage through your external engagement activities. They are often very creative and ideational. They will innovate and create opportunities to support businesses, large and small. Simplifying workflow processes is a key priority for universities post-pandemic, reducing bureaucracy and improving efficiency. 5th generation universities will need highly capable leaders and managers, who are willing to take calculated risks to achieve mutual and societal benefit.

Consortia management across sectors will become an increasingly important skill for alliance professionals acting as 'boundary spanners' and 'knowledge brokers'. UCL's Director of Research Strategy and Policy, Sarah Chaytor, describes these people as 'the hidden wiring and the connective tissue in the broader research ecosystem' who occupy the 'third space' that spans the boundary between academic and traditional administrative staff in universities:

> Put slightly differently, their role is to enable the mobility of people, ideas and talents across traditional disciplinary, organisational and professional boundaries. They are hybrid professionals of the highest order in

the sense that they blend external expertise with academic insight – and this boundary-spanning capacity is itself often the result of a "'braided career' that has allowed the individual to experience a range of research-related environments.[32]

These 'hybrid professionals of the highest order' are an emerging group of university staff who often bring experience from other sectors such as industry, government and the voluntary sector. Boundary spanners often have extensive personal networks across multiple sectors that can help facilitate engagement with companies.

We prefer not to use the term 'third space' as it implies a lower priority than the other two traditional spaces of research and education. As highlighted, 5th generation universities have integrated all three 'spaces', of research, education and KE, with a strong foundation underpinned by value creation.

Alliance leaders help to glue and cement multi-sector and transdisciplinary relationships. Their role is critical to enable next generation universities to achieve their institutional mission, vision, and values. They understand the importance of good communication, governance and relationship management incorporating R&D, teaching and innovation. They liaise and coordinate internally to ensure a joined-up approach with research contracts, advancement, pre- and post-grant award teams and academics. As Sarah Chaytor said, often alliance leaders have transitioned from roles in industry or government and have in-depth knowledge of certain sectors and bring strong management, leadership, and communication skills.

Just as conservationists promote the healthy management and stewardship of natural environments, alliance professionals are conservationists and stewards of carefully managed, open university environments that promote collaboration and partnership for change.

In many university governance structures, the role of VP (Research and Innovation) is the executive office in charge of strategic research and innovation alliances. We recommend that industry experience and awareness is a great asset for such role-holders to understand the culture and drivers of industry.

These staff require entrepreneurial understanding and skills to effectively engage with academics and industry. They also require a holistic and integrated understanding of knowledge and research valorisation that sees the huge potential benefit of bringing research, education and KE together in a seamless way for external organisations approaching the university.

How to create shared value across different university functions

What are the attitudes, services and structures that lead to successful outcomes at engaging with industry in areas such as research, education and innovation? We consider the roles and strategies for university leadership, industry engagement offices, other externally facing business units, schools, departments and faculties. Universities often structure their innovation around a TTO, with central or faculty responsibilities for developing entrepreneurship programmes for staff and students.

How can you use your university procurement to your advantage to form strategic alliances with companies? Can you link procurement to research ROI and in-kind contributions? Universities should look for more from their suppliers than just procurement. How can you work together for mutual benefit? Your suppliers have talent and innovation needs. Likewise, how can you leverage your student and staff volunteering and entrepreneurial activities to foster connectivity and relationship building with external organisations including companies, charities and civil society?

In the next chapter, we will discuss our structured engagement approach that initially involves a discovery workshop to explore potential areas for collaboration to create shared value across different functions of each organisation. Table 2.6 shows how university and corporate functions interact to achieve this. The drivers for creating shared value frequently provide topics to frame initial discussions and foster peer-to-peer relationships within a 5th generation university context.

Table 2.6: How university and corporate functions interact to create shared value

University function	Corporate function	Drivers for creating shared value
Executive Leadership Team (President/Provost/Vice Provost/Dean/Vice-Dean/ Head of Department)	Executive Leadership Team (CEO, EVP [Executive Vice President], SVP [Senior Vice President], VP, MD)	Transformational strategic alliances to achieve socio-economic impact
Research/TTO	Research and Development	Thought leadership, technology pipeline to accelerate innovation, e.g. IPR/licensing, joint publications
Consultancy/Education	Corporate Development	Staff learning and development/CPD
Careers Service	Talent Acquisition/ HR	Build talent pipeline to sustain global innovation
Community Engagement	EDI (Equality, Diversity and Inclusion)/CSR/ Marketing	Brand reputation, positioning and staff volunteering opportunities
Clinical	Sales/Business Development	Commercialisation
ICT/Estates	Account Management	Digital transformation
Advancement/Fundraising	CSR/Foundation	Enabling positive change
Alliances, Innovation and Enterprise	Alliances/Strategy/ Board	KE, mutual benefit, growth and impact
Procurement	Sales and Marketing	Innovation, prestige projects that will interest the whole sector and have high visibility
Legal, Research Services, Contracting	Legal, Contracting	Reviewing and closing framework agreements, NDAs, MoUs (Memorandums of Understanding) etc

Equality, diversity and inclusion

At the start of 2021, fewer than 1 per cent – just 140 out of 22,000 – professors in the UK were black.[33] Globally, barely more than one fifth of all university vice-chancellors and only 3 in 50 of those at the top universities are women,[34] yet the first person to win two Nobel Prizes was a woman – Marie Curie – and to this day, she is the only person to win the Nobel Prize in two scientific fields.

5th generation universities will greatly value equality, diversity and inclusion (EDI) and be able to deliver world-class, sector-leading transformation in this area. They will recognise the link between EDI and better innovation and will form alliances with those committed to similar values. They will look to spur initiatives to build capacity across sectors for growing a new diversity of leaders from a wider range of backgrounds than ever before, including a greater diversity of academic entrepreneurs.

Wise industry and academic leaders recognise that there is far more talent outside their own organisations globally than within them and seek to collaborate through an open innovation approach to access this 'talent ocean' of inspirational creativity and entrepreneurial drive. This means engaging in both programmatic activity like student projects and internships as well as philanthropic initiatives like funding scholarships for under-represented student groups. 5th generation universities in the Global North and Global South will know that this means they need to collaborate through transformational academic and industry alliances more than ever before. Such alliances will seek to give more than they get to reverse the 'brain drain' and inequality of resources between different universities.

Strong university–university and university–industry interactions are vital to facilitate joint business planning towards achieving more impactful EDI activities within higher education. This means recognising together talent gaps and collaborating to source talent over workable timelines through, for example:

- joint staff appointments between Global North and Global South institutions;

- joint degree programmes delivered using digital collaboration and distance-learning platforms, and PhD internships within different countries;
- staff exchange of postdocs and academic staff.

Reducing inequality (SDG 10)

Many think the pandemic means that there must be a fundamental change of approach worldwide to tackling global inequalities. Transformational strategic alliances can make a huge contribution to reducing inequality both locally and globally through:

- promoting EDI at all levels;
- offering micro-credentials to those most marginalised via new forms of distance learning;
- collaboration as equal partners with institutions in the Global South;
- considering how to provide affordable access to knowledge and new technologies, particularly those developed through 'frugal innovation' approaches, e.g. development of a low-cost laptop;
- supporting entrepreneurs in disadvantaged parts of the world;
- raising aspirations through schools' outreach and community engagement;
- co-creation and citizen science with a clear end-user in mind for research;
- contributing to the development of accessible technologies, opening new markets and opportunities and empowering people with disabilities.

Transdisciplinary and multi-sector approach

Universities are key enablers of change and very influential with government bodies and within civil society. Multi-sector organisations need to find common goals and mutual benefits by harnessing thinking outside their own sectors to find solutions. As the world becomes increasingly urbanised, citywide transformations brought about by transformational strategic alliances and an awareness of the importance of environmental factors will start to occur at a greater pace than humanity has ever seen. A systems-engineering or systems-based approach will be very important to ensure the most effective implementation. This will require experts in many different disciplines, such as engineering, environmental design, architecture, public health, social epidemiology and behaviour science, among others.

Operationalising the UN Sustainable Development Goals

Systemic change is only brought about by individuals in different sectors of society wanting to 'be the change' themselves, to quote Gandhi and, more recently, Swedish environmental activist Greta Thurnberg, who said, "I know we need a system change rather than individual change. But you cannot have one without the other."[35]

We all have tough choices to make about how we live our lives today, either for the benefit or to the detriment of our planetary environment and future generations. These choices are driven by our motivations, shaped by our values. What values shape our contemporary culture? Consumption, materialism, but also, increasingly, a shared sense of humanity.

What is the most pressing problem that multidisciplinary research from universities could help to solve? The 2018 report from the Intergovernmental Panel on Climate Change (IPCC) predicts the impacts of a 1.5° rise in global temperature above pre-industrial levels with a view to 'strengthening the global response to the threat of climate change, sustainable development, and efforts to eradicate poverty'.[36] Climate change disproportionately affects the world's poorest.[37] How can billions of tonnes of CO_2 emissions per year be removed from the Earth's atmosphere? How can carbon emissions be drastically reduced and replaced in a new zero-carbon economy? Transitioning to a more sustainable future will require mobilisation and transformation of quintuple helix-aware alliances on an unprecedented scale. This will enable innovative solutions to be developed at pace to address climate change.

Over 130 countries have declared they want to achieve net-zero-carbon emissions by 2050. Many similar pledges have also been made across different sectors, including academia. How can university and business leaders tackle the climate emergency and operationalise all the UN SDGs, so that shared values lead to real change? What can your university do today to start to chip away at the SDGs through behaviour change, collaborative research, teaching and KE, including shaping public policy at different levels?

5th generation universities will get their own house in order in terms of locally based changes that drive a more sustainable campus. They will also contribute to more sustainable university towns and cities that seek to respond to the UN SDGs effectively within their own local context. Many UK universities have been trialling more environmentally sustainable transport models for students commuting around campus. For example, a trial of electric scooters has been rolled out across Salford University recently. During the trial, 80,000 individual trips have been taken by 30,000 unique riders covering 100,000 miles, mostly close to Manchester city centre.[38] This is a small step in the right direction. How can your institution respond to the challenge of climate change and support students to learn, act and lead for sustainability in the transition towards zero-carbon campuses? It will inevitably need strong transdisciplinary collaboration including Social Sciences, Humanities and Arts (SSHA) and STEM disciplines, working with external partners in the community.

Professor Jim Longhurst is the Chair of the Alliances for Sustainability Leadership in Education within the Environmental Association for Universities and Colleges (EAUC). He recommends climate action toolkits to help senior leadership teams in universities.[39] This includes a Sustainability Leadership Scorecard for self-assessment of where universities' strengths and weaknesses lie. The Scorecard can be used to develop a gap analysis action plan that will help to protect biodiversity, work towards climate and social justice, and lower campus greenhouse gas emissions.

For 5th generation universities, sustainability is integral to all their activities: their teaching, research and innovation are all underpinned by effective engagement. 'Living Labs' have become increasingly common for universities to promote and deploy, enabling students to gain exposure to real-world challenges and providing them with an opportunity to learn the multidisciplinary skills needed to create viable solutions. Lifecycle analysis, systems thinking and circular economy are all important skills for students to develop. Often students use these lab environments to develop Proof of Concepts (PoCs) or working prototypes. These solution demonstrators can be a very useful 'shop window' for visitors from industry to see and learn about a university's capabilities. They can help to pave the way for a strategic alliance.

There are encouraging signs that across sectors there is a growing desire to collaborate to address the many challenges facing our world. The Engineering Research Visioning Alliance (ERVA) is an effort to help identify and develop bold and transformative new engineering research directions. Funded by the US Government's National Science Foundation (NSF), ERVA is a diverse, inclusive and engaged partnership that convenes and enables an array of voices to address national, global and societal needs through high-impact, cross-domain research. ERVA's mission is to identify bold new engineering research directions that meet the following criteria:

- they are capable of major societal impact;
- they involve broad engagement of the engineering research community;
- they address national and global challenges;
- they are capable of catalysing the engineering research community.

Although not limited to these examples, they reference the 17 UN SDGs, alongside:

- NSF's 10 Big Ideas[40]
- National Academy of Engineering's 14 Grand Challenges[41]

The initiative is managed by the UIDP, a professional association focused on strengthening university–industry partnerships.[42]

Similar governmental, and ideally intergovernmental, initiatives worldwide have the potential to bring universities, industry and civil society together to find ideas that will unite all parties in tackling global challenges. Mission-led roadmaps for cutting-edge research can lead to significant impacts for our world.

5th generation university leaders will look to form multi-sector collaborations on new ventures that offer 'millions of sustainable innovations' as per Sir David Attenborough's COP26 speech, addressing the future of areas such as:

- Transport especially air travel and shipping
- Land use, including agriculture
- Energy generation and supply to homes and businesses
- Waste and recycling
- Tackling biodiversity loss
- Nature-based solutions
- Interactions between animal, human and environmental health
- CO_2 removal and reduction of carbon footprint across multiple industries

Each of these issues must be translated into research themes for further exploration and innovation by 5th generation universities.

Wise, courageous, collaborative leadership and solutions

There is no doubt that both cross-sector (university-to-university) and multi-sector alliances boost impact. To achieve great impact, great vision is required. US President John F. Kennedy famously said in 1961, "I believe that this nation should commit itself to achieving the goal, before this decade is out, of landing a man on the Moon and returning him safely to the Earth."[43]

Achieving the UN SDGs will require similar vision, as well as wise, thoughtful, collaborative, and creative leadership and solutions. Are your leadership facilitating new thinking and vision around realising your institutional mission and strategy, and are they willing to collaborate with others to make this a reality?

Should SDG solutions be led by industry, university, governmentor community? What communities really want is not necessarily what scientists and engineers or politicians think they should have. No new technology will be effective unless it has widespread community acceptance and take-up. Understanding the real needs of local communities in the poorest parts of the world is vital and charities and civil society have great experience here. There is a whole movement focused on small-scale, appropriate technology. Circular economy approaches popularised and pioneered by British sailor Ellen MacArthur are very important for a more sustainable future.[44]

Leaders in 5th generation universities will be concerned about what skills their graduates will need to acquire for the life in the digitally enabled, agile workforce of the 21st century, alongside just a degree. They frequently consider how higher education can be transformed to meet the needs of tomorrow's workforce. We argue that transformational strategic alliances can facilitate the necessary changes, particularly at the regional scale through inclusive partnerships between city regions and local government bodies covering apprenticeships, internships and work-based learning opportunities, for example. Altogether, such initiatives will aim to make graduates ready for careers in both industry and academia, or in other sectors.

Albert Einstein demonstrated in physics the equivalence of mass and energy through his famous formula $E = mc^2$.[45] Strong and large-scale quintuple relationships have the necessary magnitude and critical mass to leverage co-investment and release the energy necessary to achieve positive change, both locally and globally. 5th generation universities in both the Global North and the Global South will work together to ensure greater engagement in and through their research, teaching and innovation. Such universities will be pioneers who are willing to experiment, occasionally make mistakes, but learn quickly and pivot where necessary. They will then adapt their engagement models to maximise societal benefit and impact. They will promote a continuous learning culture where mutual respect, understanding and trusted relationships with allies are highly valued.

Economic recovery and 'levelling up' through regional and transformational strategic alliances

How can universities help companies to recover from the impact of the pandemic to innovate and build business resilience against future shocks? As firms restructure, investing in R&D to harness new opportunities in both the knowledge and wellbeing economies will be vital for survival. Companies are learning about the business benefits of new technologies, automating processes, using AI to predict client behaviour, and implementing cloud solutions. In certain areas of technology, there is currently a 'war on talent', particularly in global cities with a growing tech community, like London. Leading Computer Science departments are facing an exodus of staff into wealthy technology companies that offer better salaries and stimulating research environments. Companies are investing in recruiting new talent and seek to build links with the wider innovation ecosystem in their regions and internationally.

Increasingly governments around the world expect universities to help to address regional economic disparities, raise productivity and drive efficiency and innovation activity in their regions. Governments' role is to enable the environment for multi-sector alliances to flourish. They do this by acting as a facilitator and cross-fertiliser of these. In our view, it is not the role of governments to 'level up', rather they empower universities, industry, the voluntary sector and entrepreneurs to do levelling up in their cities and regions, as they tackle UN SDGs such as ending global poverty through technological and social innovation. Successful government initiatives driving multi-sector alliance formation at both regional and national levels include the Connecting Capabilities Fund (CCF)[46] and sector-focused Catapults in the UK.[47] In the US, the corresponding initiatives would include the work of the NSF and the drive towards regional technology hubs.

5th generation universities understand the power of place and the importance of civic engagement.[48] They form alliances with local government and civil society groups to work on both local and global challenges together, becoming leading partners with their cities and regions in resilience and innovation, helping to boost post-COVID-19 recovery. In the UK, this increasingly involves universities coordinating innovation activity on behalf of Local Economic Partnerships (LEPs) so that industry in their regions can be more effective at R&D and can help with the 'Levelling-Up' agenda of tackling regional wealth disparities.[49]

This agenda or approach is rooted in the concept of 'smart specialisation strategy' that aims to achieve a more inclusive and globally competitive regional economy by ensuring research and innovation support is tailored to the knowledge-based industries that have significant potential or critical mass in terms of capabilities and competencies. Universities are seen as 'anchor institutions' that are vital in supporting the regional entrepreneurial ecosystem.[50] While this is good and aligns with a 4th generation university approach, in our view, smart

Figure 2.2: The roles of government, 5th generation universities and industry in economic development to address UN SDGs

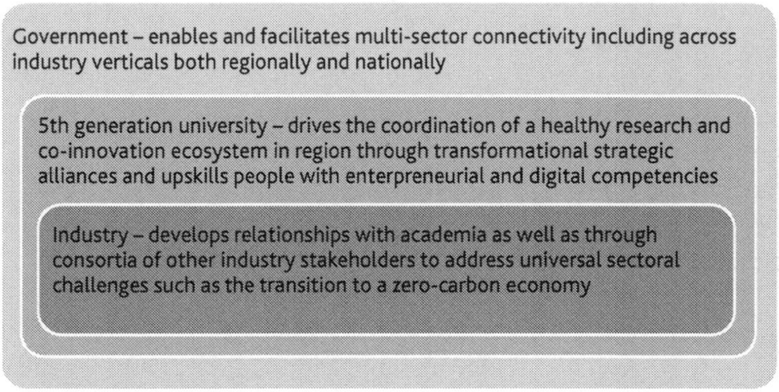

Government – enables and facilitates multi-sector connectivity including across industry verticals both regionally and nationally

5th generation university – drives the coordination of a healthy research and co-innovation ecosystem in region through transformational strategic alliances and upskills people with enterpreneurial and digital competencies

Industry – develops relationships with academia as well as through consortia of other industry stakeholders to address universal sectoral challenges such as the transition to a zero-carbon economy

specialisation strategies must recognise that university KE is about far more than just technology transfer.

In contrast, 5th generation universities recognise that the regional anchor role of a university means building up and equipping people with new skills, including entrepreneurship, that can lead to social innovation, rather than just developing and commercialising new technologies. Such universities are open to working in a collaborative manner with industry in their region to achieve positive change for wider society (Figure 2.2).

Disruption will reshape higher education

Corporate leaders with foresight recognise that the average lifespan of companies is decreasing significantly and only those that adopt to the rapidly changing social, economic, environmental and technological conditions will survive. The average lifespan of a company listed in the S&P 500 Index of leading US companies has decreased by more than 50 years in the past century, from

67 years in the 1920s to just 15 years in 2012, according to Professor Richard Foster from Yale University.[51]

Industry sectors today are facing disruption from an array of new technologies, including advanced computing and materials science, applied AI, and future connectivity. New start-ups in these areas can now rapidly become 'unicorns' with a billion-dollar market valuation.[52] According to data from Dealroom, as of 2021, Europe is ahead of China in the number of unicorns created, and the UK is leading the increase, driven by fintech, life science and healthcare, blockchain, cleantech and autonomous cars.[53] Germany and France are second and third in Europe. However, the US is still significantly in the lead.[54] The appetite for venture capital in some university towns such as Oxford is booming, almost doubling over the course of 2021. Evidence suggests that the winning formula for deep tech start-ups is to focus on attracting the best R&D talent and attracting investors willing to fund a long R&D phase known as 'patient' capital.[55]

London, Cambridge and Oxford (known as the UK's 'Golden Triangle' universities) are home to numerous successful incubator and accelerator programmes, including many led or initiated by universities. These include IDEALondon, ConceptionX, Oxford Foundry (OxFo) and Cambridge Cluster.[56] We have seen a growing trend in leading universities enabling a 'wave' of positive change for other universities both nationally and globally to 'surf together' on through collaboration. This trend is likely to accelerate through the activity of visionary KE practitioners and university leaders with a focus on finding solutions to the UN SDGs by tapping into diverse global talent pools of academic and student entrepreneurs (Figure 2.2).

New industries are being unleashed and are in their infancy. Digital transformation requires universities, like other organisations, to consider their cloud strategy and how AI, behavioural analytics and blockchain may impact their business models. It is also reshaping academic disciplines, with AI influencing social sciences and the humanities. Diverse industries, including higher education, are being reshaped and there is a trend for service sector companies – for example finance, retail, legal, insurance, transport, shipping and energy – to build 'tech' innovation structures to capitalise on the data science R&D ecosystem.

Nurturing start-ups among your staff and students and seeking to grow the entrepreneurial ecosystem in your region should be a key priority for any 5th generation university. Your university's impact management system should measure the value that these start-ups and spinouts are creating, not just in financial terms, but also in alignment with achieving the UN SDGs. Universities in the Global South will also increasingly set up incubators and accelerators to drive innovation in their regions, helping to translate innovative and appropriate technology solutions from research into society to achieve positive change. Forward-thinking Global North Universities can collaborate to help make this a success.

Tool: UN Sustainable Development Goals engagement canvas for alignment assessment

If you wish to create, release and realise value from your university partnerships (co-value creation), then alignment, particularly around your institution's vision, mission and values, is vital. Our canvas tool (Table 2.7) offers a planning and prioritisation matrix (which can be used interchangeably by both universities and industry). It can help university leaders assess the alignment of their university with a potential industry partner through the lens of the UN SDGs. It enables universities to:

- map opportunities for co-value creation against partner assets and their complementarity with your university's strategic priorities;
- consider the likely societal impact to be generated through a potential alliance;
- explore and envision potential multidisciplinary research challenge themes for an alliance, drawing on institutional strengths as well as industry domains or use cases that could be relevant;
- achieve the right balance between proactive creativity to foster new alliances that align with your university's strategic direction, while considering risk management in relation to innovation and engagement.

Table 2.7: UN SDG engagement canvas for university–industry alignment assessment

Industry ally:	Created by:
Date:	Version:

ALLIANCE OBJECTIVE

In one sentence, explain how a strategic alliance with industry will help you achieve your university's vision, mission, and values, linked to the UN SDGs? *Mention specific UN SDGs here and in each section below.*

CULTURE	INTERNAL CAPABILITIES	IMPACT
Teaching alignment – how can your curriculum delivery be enhanced through this alliance?	*Research alignment* – taking both the global and local perspective into account, what do you believe are the three most critical challenges for multi-disciplinary research in your institution to solve linked to the UN SDGs?	*Innovation/KE alignment* – from the perspective of your region and nation, and in consultation with government bodies, what do you believe are the three most critical problems to address that will achieve the greatest impact?

COMPLEMENTARITY	OPPORTUNITIES	RISKS
List complementary assets of industry partner here that can accelerate your progress towards addressing these global and local (glocal) challenges.	List opportunities for co-value creation here.	List potential risks resulting from this engagement and how these could be managed/mitigated. What is your institution's risk appetite?

ALIGNMENT EVALUATION

What Key Results will be most useful to gauge the success of this alliance in 3–5 years' time? This should be used in conjunction with the metrics in your university's VSEM (Table 2.1).

It also provides a short internal vision-sharing document to build internal support in your department, faculty or institution for an alliance.

Case study: National Science Foundation Convergence Accelerator – an example of a government-led programme facilitating the emergence of 5th generation universities

This US government initiative is a great example of the future of government-led, multidisciplinary and multi-sector research and innovation funding focused on addressing societal challenges that will encourage universities to orientate their focus towards transformational strategic alliances for positive change. The programme is focused on a convergent research approach that:

- is use-inspired and application-oriented;
- is fed by basic research and discovery;
- integrates teams from industry, academia, non-profits, government and other communities of practice;
- offers intensive hands-on education and mentorship to participants.

Project teams representing a mix of disciplines, expertise and organisations from academia, industry, non-profits, government, philanthropic foundations, and other communities of practice and sectors are formed. Such cross-cutting partnerships offer researchers and innovators the opportunity to accelerate their research towards tangible solutions that make a difference. Through an intense and hands-on journey, researchers gain skills and experiences that are applied during the programme and throughout their career.

The programme recognises that national-scale societal challenges cannot be solved by a single discipline. Instead, these challenges require convergence: the merging of innovative ideas, approaches and technologies from a wide and diverse range of sectors and expertise.

Launched in 2019, the NSF Convergence Accelerator (see Figure 2.3) builds upon basic research and discovery to accelerate solutions towards societal impact. The programme funds teams to solve societal challenges through convergence research and innovation. To enhance its impact, the Accelerator also places

Figure 2.3: The key features of the National Science Foundation Convergence Accelerator

Multidisciplinary approach

- Funded teams are composed of diverse disciplines, expertise and organisations.
- Teams merge ideas and share approaches and techniques to speed use-inspired solutions toward real-world application.
- Teams have no size limits and are expected to evolve as a project advances.

Societal impact

- Funded projects are intentionally focused on sustainability and national-scale impact.
- At the end of the fixed three-year term, teams are expected to provide high-impact deliverables that address societal challenges and enhance the nation's competitiveness and security.

Cross-cutting partnerships

- Catalysed partnerships strengthen each funded effort by providing end-user insights, resources, services, infrastructure and transition-to-practice pathways.

Innovation curriculum

- Provides teams with the tools to move from idea to proof of concept, to prototype and then solution.
- Researchers gain knowledge in human-centred design, team science, communication, and storytelling and pitching.

Coopetition environment

- A 'coopetition' environment stimulates innovative ideas.
- Funded teams compete and share expertise and resources to assist solutions in advancing to the next phase.

Track alignment

- Phase 2 teams collaborate on integration with other teams within their convergent research track – ensuring the track's focus is more impactful than each individually funded effort.

Source: National Science Foundation

teams together in cohorts, synergising their work through facilitated collaboration.

While the overarching goal of the programme is to enable long-lasting societal impact, results for each solution and the way a solution transitions to societal impact will vary. Examples include:

- integration of a solution into existing systems;
- production of open-source tools and knowledge products;
- expansion of a solution into new markets;
- follow-on funding and investment.

Lessons learned

- 5th generation universities are:
  - industry-engaged through their institutional strategies;
  - ambitious for positive change for societal benefit and the public good of humanity. This shapes an integrated and multifaceted approach to their research, teaching and innovation activity, including their approach to technology transfer. They seek to educate their students to become more globally aware citizens;
  - 'place-based' in their thinking around innovation, aware of both their geographical context as a hub for entrepreneurship as well as how the local can shape the global. They help entrepreneurs in their local community who are seeking positive change, even if they are not directly part of their university;
  - passionate about EDI – equality, diversity and inclusion. These values shape their approach to talent acquisition, with a desire to build capacity through strengthening collaborative networks that expand the talent ocean rather than accelerating the 'brain drain';
  - SDG- or 'Grand Challenge'-focused through their mission, vision and values;
  - multifaceted, proactive and holistic in their approach to external engagement, looking to create win–win alliances that cover education, research, innovation and KE, and to achieve both mutual and societal benefit. This means that they do not just focus on growing spinouts, just to tick boxes of government requirements, rather they look to grow student projects with industry and demonstrate a more nuanced understanding of KE. Such alliances require cross-institutional external engagement units to work together, even if they are within distributed teams. They will operate as one overlay function or proxy, so that industry allies have a coherent and coordinated interaction with the whole university;
  - utilise all their assets and brand, commercialisation capability (for example, through technology transfer and entrepreneurship), infrastructure and Alliance Capacity

(AC) to maximise positive change through targeting the UN SDGs in transdisciplinary, multifaceted transformational strategic alliances;

- maintain an institutional record of 'Lessons Learned' as well as 'Benefits Realised' for each strategic alliance. This could be held within a CRM so that tacit knowledge is not lost and is a mark of an effective learning organisation;

- empower all staff, particularly those who work in external engagement roles, to value alliances as being fundamental to achieving both positive change in the world and their institutional mission. They offer services to help steward companies well to the end goal of 'transformation'.

• Alignment between university and industry cannot happen effectively until the university is aligned and integrated internally. This requires strong governance policies to be in place for handling negotiations of multi-dimensional Master Research Agreements, for example, as well as ownership of IPR and handling conflicts of interest.

• Growing consultancy opportunities and innovation around social enterprise business models offer a good model for engaging with researchers from social sciences, arts and humanities backgrounds, particularly. The creation of new accelerators for KE across these disciplines is a key priority for 5th generation universities.

• Working with industry does not have to be a threat to academic freedom provided expectations and boundaries are discussed early on in engagements in a respectful, open and transparent manner. Boundaries concerning IP and costs for licensing in sponsored research agreements should be highlighted at the start of the discussions.

• Governments can play a key enabling role in catalysing and encouraging behaviour change. They can provide funding within the higher education sector to form cross-cutting, multi-sector transformational alliances to address the UN SDGs via a challenge and mission-driven approach. This should include piloting novel business model innovation related to creating more inclusive, equitable higher educational opportunities for all (SDG 4). This will require universities to provide more training and incentives for staff to engage in 'team science', 'frugal innovation', and KE with industry and other partners within government (whether local or central), academia (particularly between Global North and Global South) and civil society, for example charities and NGOs.

- Within the UK context, the KEF metrics and Concordat provide a very good facilitator for behaviour change though this is just the beginning.[57] 5th generation universities will seek to grow expectations and understanding of the importance of KE activities and valorisation. They will combine this with staff incentives and reward and recognise staff contribution towards positive change brought about by such activities, whether from academic or professional services staff.

- Governments have an important role as enablers, facilitators and brokers of collaboration and knowledge exchange. The concept of 'smart specialisation strategy' is increasingly influencing a multi-sector approach to innovation focused on regional economic development, addressing wealth disparities and inequality. However, we are concerned that the concept sees KE in a purely instrumentalist fashion, for driving economic growth, rather than a more holistic understanding of societal benefit and the good of humanity.

- The NSF Convergence Accelerator offers a catalytic approach to helping universities see the benefits of multi-sector collaboration to solving grand challenges. Experimentation through team science and a lean entrepreneurship approach to research and development offer ways to change mindsets and stimulate positive change by testing ideas quickly and finding solutions. Many partnerships include diverse participants from corporates, start-ups and the not-for-profit sector and cover issues such as the future of work and how quantum computation, AI and data science may affect both employees and employers.

3

Developing and managing alliances

Action without vision is only passing time, vision
without action is merely daydreaming, but vision with
action can change the world.

Joel Arthur Barker[1]

'Collaborate' comes from the Latin verb 'collaborare', 'col'
meaning 'together' and 'laborare' meaning 'to work'. So how
is 'working together' through transdisciplinary partnership for
positive change done? How are transformational strategic alliances
initiated with companies and factored or 'baked in' from the
outset? How can you integrate industry insights and input within
your educational programmes most effectively? This chapter
explores how 5th generation universities will learn the skills
needed to achieve positive change for society, through alliances,
at speed and scale. They do this by effectively developing and
managing their alliances through alignment of priorities, by
building capacity and combining flexibility and focus.

Collaborative, competitor and industry intelligence

Before 5th generation universities, whether in the Global
North or Global South, can develop formal relationships with
prospective industry allies, they will gather useful collaborative
intelligence. How does your university gain intelligence about
your competitive and collaborative environment, including
both private and public sector innovation within your region?
5th generation universities will not only gather intelligence but
also contribute to the creation of actionable insight for partners

within their region including local government, community and industry stakeholders. Universities can engage with the branches of their respective rural, city, regional or state government responsible for economic growth, regeneration and innovation. Working with economic development units within government bodies is an effective way for universities to learn about regional skill requirements, ambitions, international links, and funding opportunities that will attract industry partners to their regions (see Figure 3.1).

Your university should have awareness of your immediate market opportunities including which corporate R&D labs, university-led accelerators, incubators and venture capital funders are operating in your area. How this is defined will vary, since a large research-intensive university may have a global brand, whereas a smaller, teaching-focused institution may have a more localised reach.

Alongside intelligence about university competitors, it is vital for 5th generation university corporate engagement teams to gain industry intelligence. A data-centric approach to industry intelligence should form part of your institution's 'foresight strategy'. This enables universities to map the current and future environment of trendsetters and influencers in the corporate world so they can be more effective in their partner selection, and would include intelligence to answer questions like:

- How do your internal capabilities align with gaps in company needs? (For this, you will need to find out what research and innovation is already happening at your institution that would be of interest to a particular 'prospect' company.)
- What technology areas are current hot and emerging topics of interest?
- What corporate initiatives, either programmatic or philanthropic, are most likely to align with your institution's activities and core research capabilities?
- Which companies are likely to be most impactful at addressing the UN SDGs, and why?

How can you develop an innovation 'radar' for your prospective alliances with industry? One place to start is by gaining external

Figure 3.1: How to leverage industry intelligence to improve your external engagement through 'orchestrated serendipity'

Data gathering – utilise both offline and online resources including your university library and library experts, online patent libraries, advancement researchers, data-mining experts and government data sources

Corporate intelligence (knowledge and insight)

Orchestrated serendipity – informed, timely opportunities for targeted engagement and outreach to demonstrate university capabilities (business development)

Alliance management – new impactful strategic alliances formed or existing alliances strengthened through relevant engagement intelligence from government innovation strategy policy documents, think tanks, technology consultancies and academic 'megatrend' reports. These normally make predictions that look five to ten years ahead. They help forward-thinking university leaders and alliance leaders to spot opportunities for innovative collaborations that others miss.

In our experience, universities are generally slow to make use of corporate data and intelligence in managing their alliance activity. This is probably due to a lack of understanding of the value such information can provide for corporate engagement as well as for strategic corporate philanthropy. 5th generation universities will recognise the enormous value that such data can provide and will wish to leverage the collection and insights derived from this data to make their KE and engagement practices more effective, achieving greater mutual and societal benefit in the process. In gathering, recording (for example, through a CRM) and utilising such intelligence, combined with timely and proactive communications with prospective partners, 5th generation universities can, to some extent, create their own 'orchestrated' serendipity and achieve transformational strategic alliances (see Figure 3.1).

As well as external intelligence, internal intelligence data dashboards are very useful, providing a summary of your institution's 'footprint' through mission areas such as research, education, innovation and economic development towards achieving the UN SDGs. They should record information on joint publications with industry partners, for example. They should also help to capture the engagement of alumni advocates who can act as corporate champions and make a 'warm introduction' to prospective companies. Well-informed business development and KE professionals are more impressive to colleagues in industry than those who have not done their research. This approach can be particularly effective when used with digital collaboration tools to save time on travel and enable engagement with a greater number of companies.

Innovation and KE requires taking some risks in trying new approaches to engage with companies where there may be opportunities to realise mutual and societal benefit in the mid- to long term (the next three to five years). This requires

university leaders to understand that ROI through philanthropic donations and new sponsored research contracts will take time to materialise. However, investing in growing your strategic alliance and industry intelligence functionality is a way to build resilience and future-proof your institution. 5th generation universities have moved on from a transactional and tactical approach to a more collaborative, bespoke, strategic, and relational one.

Useful resources for industry intelligence-gathering include:

- Pitchbook – a source of information on start-ups and acquisitions;[2]
- Crunchbase – a source of general business intelligence, company insights from early-stage start-ups to Fortune 1000 companies;[3]
- LinkedIn Sales Navigator – useful for finding alumni in companies who can provide warm introductions;[4]
- Request for Proposal (RFP) services, for example Grant Forward;[5]
- Google alerts – easily create customised news alerts to monitor corporates that you are interested in forging alliances with to find out what they may be interested in;[6]
- FTSE 100, Fortune 500/1000 listings and surveys of top graduate employers;
- keyword searches of investor reports related to research and technology areas alongside the UN SDGs.

Several expected technologies are likely to emerge over the next decade. Examples of how some of these would contribute to achieving the UN SDGs are:

- virus detection sensors (SDG 3)
- a hospital system fully realising remote treatment (SDG 3, 10, 11)
- energy control in autonomous cities (SDG 7, 9, 11, 12)
- digital environment for anyone to learn at any time (SDG 4, 5, 8, 9, 10, 11, 17)

As you can see, the SDGs offer a great way to consider the potential positive impact of technological change on society.

Stages of university–industry alliance development

After carrying out effective intelligence gathering, necessary due diligence, orchestrating serendipity and initiating conversations with prospective allies in industry, the next step for alliance leaders is to develop and manage these relationships. This must be done in a constructive, structured and strategic manner. There are four necessary stages in most alliance journeys: forming, storming, norming and performing, and outperforming (see Table 3.1).

Our thinking about this alliance lifecycle or journey is influenced by psychologist Bruce Tuckman's group development model,[7] first proposed in 1965, of how healthy teams form over time and, more recently, by a healthcare research study from 2017 that linked team development stages to leadership strategies.[8] We have adapted these models to highlight the necessary alliance skills required at each stage of alliance development. We think the model is a useful type of practice-based theory to reflect upon throughout an alliance, to discern your collaboration progress in a more qualitative rather than simply quantitative manner. For example, alliance leaders are wise to discern the quality of dialogue during every interaction they have with their industry allies. Successful collaborations are all about people working together through teams to achieve results that they could never achieve independently and so this model is very relevant, in our experience.

Forming

Alliance managers, like good parents, must seek to nurture the growth of the proposed alliance from small beginnings through infancy, childhood, adolescence and into adulthood. Just as good parents have a vision for their children to grow up healthy and to fulfil their potential, so alliance managers must have a vision to form and develop strategic alliances. In this chapter, we will explain further how a VSEM tool can really help at this early stage to lay the foundations for success. A vision for an alliance that can bring positive change, within your own university and your partner organisation, cannot just be held by an alliance leader but must be validated and communicated to others in their team and more widely within the university.

Table 3.1: Alliance lifecycle or journey

Alliance development stage	Management strategies	Keys to success
Forming – preparing for a successful alliance journey.	Coordination of conversations to achieve organisational readiness to engage in a seamless manner, project management, planning, prioritisation, appointment of Executive Champion (normally academic leader).	VSEM, responsiveness, right people with the right skills and attitude in distributed teams, mixture of academics and professional services staff with track record of working with industry, shared vision and values, mutual respect.
Storming – resolving tension internally/externally and dealing with barriers to alliance success.	Influencing and coaching behaviours to help industry understand academic constraints and boundaries for alliance development, for example, around IPR during legal and contracting discussions.	Building mutual trust through open and transparent conversations and flexibility on both sides. Centrally managed workflow automation of contracting process.
Norming and performing – successful execution and day-to-day maintenance of alliances.	Creative problem solving as challenges arise, proactive peer-to-peer communications and briefings. Impact management. Presentation to different stakeholders.	CRM to record interactions, visualise progress and highlight next steps. Peer-to-peer communication and governance, balanced scorecard, lessons learned and benefits realisation logs. Co-location can help build bridges and improve communication through spatial proximity.
Outperforming – growing the alliance both internally to include new departments and externally to involve other stakeholders from multiple sectors, for example, other universities and corporates, SMEs, government bodies, charities	Foresight to recognise and optimise gaps. This may include expanding the alliance to bring on board other organisations who can help achieve more through widening participation.	Recognition, reward and incentivisation. Storytelling through video case studies and sharing best practice through professional associations.

Source: Adapted from Tuckman's group development model

It is always great to meet like-minded people who have a vision for collaboration from any organisation. It is fine to know 'why' you wish to work with a particular company, but if you cannot execute this, through an effective alliance, then that is no value whatsoever. It is a bit like setting out on a journey but then not having a map or the necessary fitness levels to be able to reach your destination. This is put succinctly in a quote popular among industry leaders from the early 1900s and often attributed to Thomas Edison: "Vision without execution is hallucination."

What lays at the inception of any collaboration between universities and industry is the need for robust interaction internally from the outset. This interaction is typically between distributed external engagement teams and academics within departments and must be effectively coordinated through email, video calls and face-to-face meetings, where necessary, to gain buy-in and support to ensure effective communication with your industry collaborator. Too often, universities fail to coordinate conversations effectively, with large companies particularly, and this can cause unnecessary damage. Organisational readiness, where seamlessly compliant interfaces maintain an always-open, peer-to-peer communication channel among all stakeholders, is a key success factor for any strategic alliance to prevail.

Having said that, the development of a long-term university–industry alliance is always a two-way street where both the university and industry must address what specifically needs to be done on both sides. To achieve a fruitful, efficient and sustainable alliance, both organisations need to have an effective and embedded alliance functionality to explore, identify and forge alliances, as well as an Executive Champion. This Champion will, as mentioned in Chapter 1, provide high-level sponsorship for the alliance, when it faces internal challenges. If one party is ready for an alliance and the other is not, then the whole initiative risks failure with reputational impact for both sides. The Executive Champion should have an unbiased and positive approach towards the benefits of working with other sectors.

During the 'forming' stage, alliance managers and leaders will develop a problem-solving and escalation path (this requires someone with strong project management skills). They will also establish a mutually agreed performance management system of key performance indicators (KPIs) to ensure the alliance stays on track. The balance scorecard tool can be very useful here. These alliance professionals will also co–develop the alliance governance structure and execution or delivery plan. There are several key roles needed for the success of alliances in this formative stage as shown in Table 3.2.

Universities should seek alliance professionals to collaborate with within industry who have prior business experience of working with academics. They should ideally have an appetite for solving societal challenges rather than a purely transactional motivation for engagement. Both sides will need to discuss their vision and specific goals or objectives for the alliance based on their organisational strategies and priorities. We recommend that you should aim to ensure alignment around no more than three overarching goals so that focus is not spread too thinly. It

Table 3.2: Peer-to-peer industry and academic roles required for strategic alliances

University roles	Industry roles
Executive Champion – typically a member of the senior leadership team, either Head of Department, Vice-Dean, Dean, Vice Provost, Provost.	Executive Champion – typically a corporate Director or above, who is a budget holder for the alliance and has authority to sign off on contracts.
Head of Academic Research/Teaching Programme, for example, Professor who will coordinate the academic side of the alliance.	Head of Business Unit, for example Head of Academic Research and Technology Partnerships.
Strategic Alliance Director – senior professional services leader who has the vision to drive forward progress of the alliance. They are the main communications lead internally across the university.	Corporate Collaboration or Research Programme Director.
Strategic Alliance Manager – acts as account manager for alliance management on a day-to-day basis. Often has good research and intelligence-gathering ability to leverage foresight and technology trend monitoring to proactively spot mutual opportunities.	Corporate Collaboration or Research Programme Manager.

is always best to start small and then scale collaborative activities with companies.

Storming

In this second stage of alliance development, the legal sign-off of the alliance takes place. This is where there can be some tensions, both internally and externally, that must be dealt with to get the agreement over the line. 5th generation universities will look to create multifaceted master collaboration or framework agreements that cover sponsored research, innovation and philanthropy, and provide room for flexibility and a diversity of future projects related to the UN SDGs, for example.

At this stage, navigating university teams such as Research Services, Contracting and Legal is essential to progress the alliance. This requires influencing and coaching behaviours on the part of the alliance team driving forward the relationship both internally and externally. Alliance leaders in universities will need to leverage their Executive Champion here to persuade academics of the relevance and importance of taking part in the necessary early-stage engagements where they will be presenting to industry partners. The Executive Champion can help to motivate and encourage busy academics to engage through appropriate incentivisation. This could involve mentioning potential PhD funding opportunities, for example, or the ability to run stimulating research and approach challenges from new perspectives. They could also mention the potential internship opportunities for their students with the corporate partner.

There will need to be open and transparent discussions covering issues such as IPR and the necessary boundaries of the alliance. Once these conversations are handled well, you will be able to grow mutual trust with your alliance partner. However, there will need to be compromise and flexibility on both sides.

Norming and performing

In this third stage, the successful day-to-day maintenance of alliances becomes central. The mutual benefits of the alliance start to be delivered as funding flows in and progress on shared objectives starts to be made. It is important that alliance managers make good use of CRM systems to record interactions, visualise progress and highlight next steps. Also, as mentioned, 5th generation universities will make use of impact management to record their progress in delivering impact related to the UN SDGs. Another tool relevant for this stage is the Balanced Scorecard, co-developed with your alliance partner so that metrics covering the most relevant KPIs for both parties are agreed. These metrics will then be reviewed at regular management board meetings, so it is important to be able to capture this information throughout.

Alliance managers must be highly responsive in their communications with their industry partner and deliver a consistently good level of customer service. This requires staff who are proactive and able to communicate well in both written and face-to-face communications. While there may occasionally be misunderstanding and miscommunication, 5th generation universities will not have a blame culture when it comes to such efforts, as long as lessons are learned quickly and the knowledge gained from such lessons is recorded and referred back to. Lessons Learned logs should then help to inform better future engagements.

At this crucial stage of organisations adjusting and 'normalising' to work (perform) together effectively through alliance structures, it is vital not to let the alliance drift. Alliance managers therefore need to be able to think creatively to solve problems and challenges that may arise, before they grow and potentially shipwreck the alliance.

Outperforming

In this final stage of alliance development, the alliance has matured, after typically around three to five years, to deliver significant positive change benefitting both organisations and wider society. The alliance has now moved beyond a transactional and even tactical engagement, to be transformational. This means it is highly effective and productive at realising and releasing benefits and impact.

Senior leadership need to recognise and celebrate mature alliances that reach this stage of development through sharing video case studies on institutional websites and social media. It is very important at this stage for the provost and president and other senior leaders to change perceptions of KE activity from being a 'third mission' or 'third stream' activity to being seen as central to enabling and supporting the whole university mission. This can help to bring about positive culture change and in turn help to move a university from a 4th to a 5th generation institution that truly values transformational alliance building for social benefit.

It is also important that alliance teams who enable progress in fulfilling the institutional vision and mission through developing and managing transformational alliances are incentivised appropriately. This includes both academic and professional services staff who contribute to making your university's alliances a real success.

Through effective governance and management processes, the alliance has demonstrated success internally and externally for both organisations. It is now time to utilise the important skill of foresight and consider whether the alliance can be broadened. This expansion could include involving new stakeholders both from within the university, for example other academic departments, or from outside the university, perhaps in other universities and corporates, or from other sectors like government or non-profits. Reasons to consider widening participation may include to:

- recognise and optimise gaps in expertise or capability;
- pivot or refocus the alliance towards other objectives;
- share best practice, including through relevant professional associations;
- grow reputation as being sector thought leaders;
- achieve even greater results including societal benefit.

For 5th generation universities, it is unlikely that well-considered alliances will ever terminate; however, they will have to evolve and adapt to changing business, political and economic conditions. Key staff involved may move on and so it is vital to consider how relationships can foster resilience so that if, for example, an important academic researcher with niche or scarce expertise leaves your university, the alliance can adapt effectively and continue. This may mean expanding or pivoting the alliance.

Alliance formation: laying the foundations through Vision, Strategy, Execution and Metrics

Every strategic alliance team and professional should have their own VSEM (as mentioned previously, this stands for Vision, Strategy, Execution and Metrics). Good use of this tool can help to ensure that the institutional vision for building alliances with industry is strategically aligned internally and operationalised effectively. In short, it can help to improve the organisational readiness of the university to make transformational strategic alliances central to the implementation of their mission.

No matter what industry you are in, or your organisation's size, strategic planning is what drives operations and ultimately makes any business grow. However, while a good strategy is vital, issues surrounding deployment often come down to effective execution. This requires the ability for alliance leaders and managers to translate clearly to their team on how to use a chosen strategy to inform their daily workload. Often congested by information clutter, many organisations in all types of industries, including higher education, have found that teams get stuck when it comes to understanding exact end goals.

So, once you and your organisation have chosen a strategy that works for your unique business, how do you properly execute it with all your team members being fully aware of the role they can play to implement strategy?

A common way of explaining the purpose of a VSEM within industry is simply 'four letters to easily organise what to do, and how to achieve a desired outcome'. Essentially this framework or tool embodies four steps that harmonise the strategy process between everyone involved. You should fill in each section of the VSEM using full sentences along with realistic timeframes and, once completed, this will provide a well-defined path for the future of your alliance development and management.

The VSEM offers a straightforward framework that encourages collaboration. Instead of long multi-page strategy documents, the VSEM is useful one-page overview. It offers a common vocabulary and process for setting and measuring goals and objectives throughout the organisation. With clear alliance planning, mobilisation of all necessary university resources for a successful alliance with an industry partner becomes easier. The VSEM enables external engagement teams within universities to:

- identify a clear purpose, a compelling direction, and a picture of what success will look like;
- identify the unique value of a team, not just in terms of individual contributions;
- help team members understand what ability or role each member brings to the alliance.

What follows is a quick elaboration of each pillar in the VSEM chart so you can streamline and structure your alliance team's operations as well as to highlight how your team will contribute to the wider institutional mission and vision. Within a university, there should be an institutional VSEM, as well as one for each external engagement team. These VSEMs should have some alignment, and we recommend they should be reviewed once per academic year.

Vision

Typically, this should be a three-to-five-year end-state goal that sets you apart from your competition. Effective leaders who expect to project a future vision they and others will follow must first address the fears that could hinder them from achieving it. Leaders establish and communicate an envisioned future state so that others can understand and support it. These leaders should not shy away from the power that comes with vision. The first step is to identify where you want to end up on your alliance journey. This is the long-term goal that everyone needs to clearly understand, support and work to make a reality.

Strategy

This should include between four and seven key actions you need to take as an organisation to achieve your vision. All you need to do is to define how you will achieve the above goal or goals. This can be the name of the strategy you are deploying, together with an outline of where resources will be used. A strategic framework is an externally facing, visual outline of activities that make up an organisation's or department's overarching strategy. A strong framework is aspirational, designed to inspire stakeholders and demonstrate how the organisation is working towards their vision, purpose or goals. Having a good strategy for deployment of anything, from new tech code in your academic research to a new business model innovation in recruitment or contracting, can ultimately lead to more efficient operations at all levels.

Execution

This section is about establishing the key short-term objectives and tactics you will need to fulfil your strategy and vision. The alliance manager should be able to clearly describe here how their team will deploy their strategy. In writing this section, you should identify and describe critical initiatives, programmes, and actions to take that will support delivery of your strategy.

Execution is taking an idea and making it happen. The execution of a plan is when you put it into effect, like the execution on the field of a football team's game plan. It can also mean the style in which a project is carried out, like a ballet's creative execution of a story.

Metrics

This is where you acknowledge results and detail who will be accountable for the execution of each step of the outlined plan. Measuring the results through metrics will help keep your alliance on track.

Figure 3.2 provides an example VSEM chart that was prepared for one of the top-ranking universities in the world who were looking to expand their corporate engagement as part of their institutional mission. There are four concurrently aligned strands of operations across the four sections of Vision, Strategy, Execution and Metrics. You can also see that the VSEM shows how different sources of revenue are recognised in the Strategy section covering research, donation, innovation and enterprise.

Figure 3.2: Example Vision, Strategy, Execution and Metrics for developing and managing alliances, developed by a Strategic Alliance team

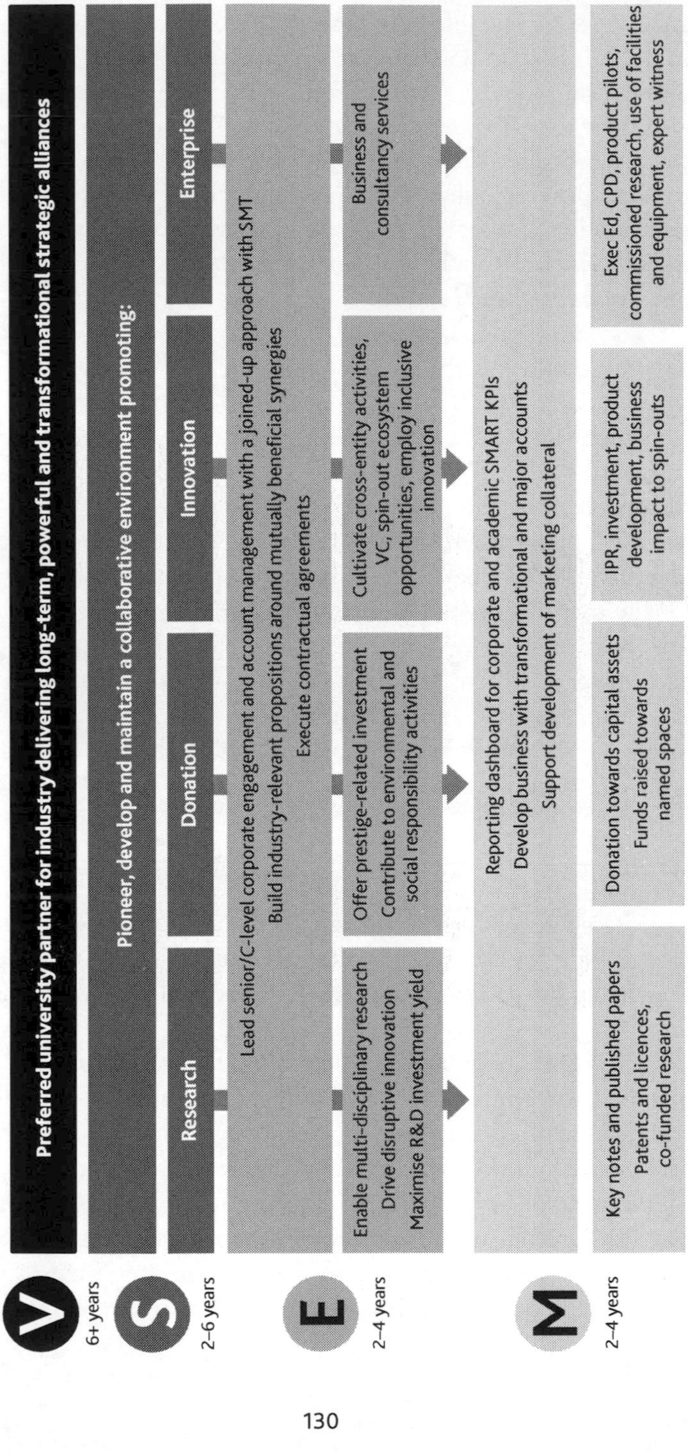

Preferred university partner for industry delivering long-term, powerful and transformational strategic alliances

V — 6+ years

S — 2–6 years

Pioneer, develop and maintain a collaborative environment promoting:

Lead senior/C-level corporate engagement and account management with a joined-up approach with SMT
Build industry-relevant propositions around mutually beneficial synergies
Execute contractual agreements

Research	Donation	Innovation	Enterprise

E — 2–4 years

Research	Donation	Innovation	Enterprise
Enable multi-disciplinary research / Drive disruptive innovation / Maximise R&D investment yield	Offer prestige-related investment / Contribute to environmental and social responsibility activities	Cultivate cross-entity activities, VC, spin-out ecosystem opportunities, employ inclusive innovation	Business and consultancy services

M — 2–4 years

Reporting dashboard for corporate and academic SMART KPIs
Develop business with transformational and major accounts
Support development of marketing collateral

Research	Donation	Innovation	Enterprise
Key notes and published papers / Patents and licences, co-funded research	Donation towards capital assets / Funds raised towards named spaces	IPR, investment, product development, business impact to spin-outs	Exec Ed, CPD, product pilots, commissioned research, use of facilities and equipment, expert witness

130

Creating a menu of institutional assets

What is your university menu of products and services (institutional assets) that you are offering to external organisations, including industry? How do you package the different mechanisms by which industry can collaborate with you to advance your institutional mission covering research, teaching and KE? Do you have an internal copywriting and marketing team who can help produce marketing collateral about this menu?

Figure 3.3 provides an example 'menu' highlighting the many ways that industry can engage with universities that they may not always be immediately aware of. We follow this with some ideas about what a typical 'menu' could look like for industry partners who may be interested in forming an alliance with your institution.

Centres of Excellence

A Centre of Excellence (CoE) is a world-class and typically co-branded centre that can be either virtual or physical in nature. It can enable focused collaboration to happen and often involves a highly motivated stakeholder team with a governance and management board providing executive sponsorship from both the university and industry partner. There is often a dedicated director to manage the centre alongside administrative support. These centres deliver pioneering research that aims to achieve transformational impact for society. A CoE brings together multidisciplinary postdocs, PhD and Masters students focusing on meeting both business priorities and societal challenges through joint research and co-innovation. In other words, a CoE is a vehicle to provide leadership, best practice, research, support and training for a specific sector.

Executive Education

Executive education (ExecEd) often refers to academic programmes at a graduate level that can lead to certification. Executive training is designed to help build business acumen, knowledge and skills and to help retain and develop staff within a company. ExecEd is often

Figure 3.3: Example of an institutional 'menu' of the many university assets that industry may not always be aware of

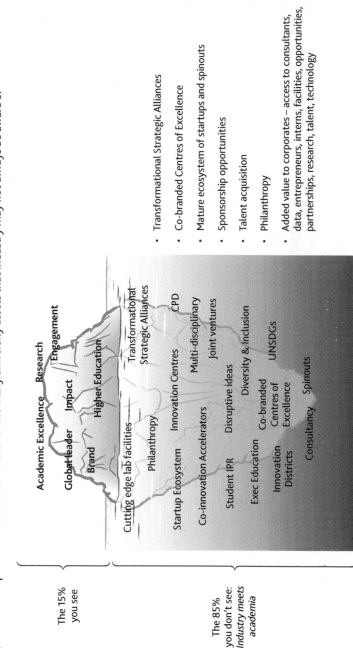

coordinated and managed through a university's consultancy arm and can often be part of the Continuous Professional Development (CPD) programmes the university will offer. A good market for your ExecEd is your alumni network.

Talent acquisition and student placements

Universities are very attractive to corporate talent acquisition teams who are interested in sourcing, attracting, interviewing, hiring and onboarding talented future staff. The university's careers service can support corporates to find the most suitable people for graduate internship programmes and employment opportunities. Talent acquisition tends to focus on long-term human resource planning to find appropriate candidates for positions that require a very specific skillset such as, most recently, AI and ML.

Additionally, work placements and internships for students are also a very important area of collaboration between university and industry. Quality placements must be linked to either study goals through student projects or long-term career plans. A placement year or internship can give students experience and inspiration for final-year projects and dissertations. It can also help to develop their soft skills, such as being able to work in a team and the ability to solve complex problems, which are valuable assets for both their academic and professional careers. A good student placement programme can easily give mutual benefit to the corporates to hire the best talent and can boost the employability and reputation of the university.

Strategic corporate philanthropy

Strategic corporate philanthropy typically refers to generally unrestricted financial donations that companies will give to universities. It can also be provided through staff volunteering within companies as a way of giving back to society. Universities benefit from philanthropy not only through additional funding for research activities or new buildings, for example, but also to provide scholarships for talented students from non-privileged or under-represented backgrounds.

In return for philanthropic funding, universities will seek to steward donors by maintaining regular communication about what their funding has achieved and will honour donors by offering to provide named spaces on campus such as a new lab, classroom, lecture hall, cafe, part of a building or a whole building. Named spaces on campus can help raise brand awareness for companies and can provide a useful source of funds for universities to improve their teaching facilities, for example. Alongside named spaces, industry may also be interested in sponsoring events such as a public lecture series, as well as academic posts, bursaries and student prizes.

Scholarships may be funded as part of a company's CSR programme. Companies engage with CSR to raise their public image and enhance their reputation. Working with companies on CSR programmes will involve significant cooperation with the company, as well as with your local community and other not-for-profit organisations. Companies should see CSR as a type of social investment that provides direct societal benefit and helps a company to become a better, more sustainable organisation that its employees can be proud of.

Finally, your menu of assets could include offering the opportunity for Funded Chairs, where a professor is recruited to work in a particular domain of strategic interest to the company. A Chair can help to provide a useful linkage between the company and university that will help to grow a transformational strategic alliance between your university and industry. While the Chair is an employee of the university, they become a bridgehead into the university for the corporate, in terms of growing their talent pipeline and wider engagement with the university. The university benefits from the strengthening of its research capabilities in a particular domain that they wish to grow, too.

Creating and nurturing trust: a stewardship approach

Alliances are living entities – they have a lifecycle and need to be nourished and managed. They don't need to last forever. They require trust that takes time to develop. We recommend frequently asking yourself questions like:

- What can I do today that will help build trust with Company X?
- How can I serve and steward Company X in a way that will improve trust by one per cent?

The former Performance Director of the highly successful British Olympic Cycling team Sir David Brailsford promoted the innovative philosophy of 'marginal gains' or the '1% factor': 'The whole principle came from the idea that if you broke down everything you could think of that goes into riding a bike, and then improved it by 1%, you will get a significant increase when you put them all together.'[9]

Brailsford's approach, like ours, is holistic. As well as looking at traditional components of successful industry engagements such as amounts of funding leveraged or number of co-publications, it also takes account of more intangible factors such as 'quality and openness of dialogue' and 'levels of trust'. This is a stewardship approach or attitude to multi-faceted university alliances that really values and looks after relationships with companies, for the good of wider society and to bring about positive change in the world, addressing UN SDGs. It is an attitude that seeks to cooperate rather than compete. It involves offering a 'one-stop-shop' or university 'front-of-house' service with a single point of contact providing account management and coordination. Forward-thinking companies should likewise provide a similar liaison person for universities to easily reach out to. Professional associations for universities and industry partners can help to facilitate contact between the most appropriate people to discuss alliance opportunities.

Working in an increasingly transdisciplinary and cross-border way between multi-sector partners in the Global North and Global South will not be easy for many universities. It requires significantly more effort than traditional academic collaboration in 3rd and 4th generation universities. It requires great communication, both internally and externally. However, if all parties have the right attitude and approach, anything is possible. Creating and nurturing trusted relationships will be key for a 5th generation university.

Ten principles for building strong alliances

How can your university or corporate start to make real progress towards building strategic alliances that address the UN SDGs? Figure 3.4 summarises the ten key principles that are the most important elements, skills and practices needed to create deep and sustainable industry partnerships that can be applied across diverse innovation and KE ecosystems.

We then discuss these principles in detail, with corresponding tools and tactics that enable the effective planning and development of transformational strategic alliances. As stated, these alliances will become a defining feature of 5th generation universities. We have found these useful in achieving effective corporate relationships in our own professional experience. We have also benchmarked these principles against best practice among KE professionals worldwide through membership of professional associations.

Start with why – alignment around shared vision, values and goals

What is the shared problem that you are trying to solve? Do you share common interests around research and innovation, for example, and have complementary expertise to solve the problem that needs to be addressed? Never compromise on your values;

Figure 3.4: Ten principles for building transformational strategic alliances

Complementarity	• Shared vision, values, interest • Mutual benefit • Partner selection • Grow trust
Communication	• Regular, effective • Testbeds • Measure • Customer journey
Culture	• Entrepreneurial/flexible • Co-location

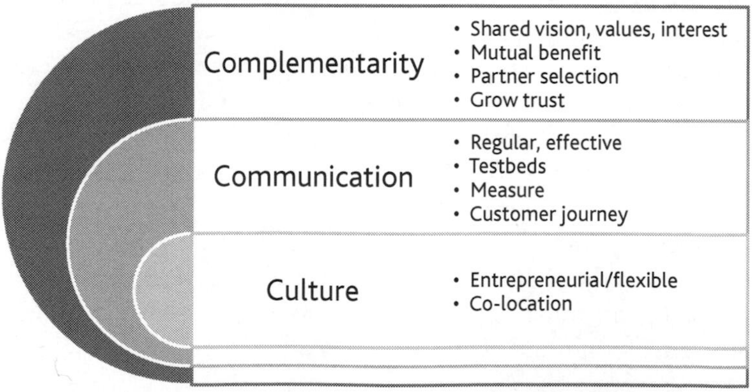

rather, look for how you can achieve more by working together across different sectors to fulfil your institutional mission.

Seek to understand each other's culture – what is and is not acceptable, and why. Good communication for building trust should be frequent and effective. You must be able to listen more than speak in the early days of alliance formation. This is even more important if there is no in-person meeting possible, only online conference calls.

Look for companies that will share their vision early on and who are willing to invest in the mid-term when they find the right partner, for example giving at least a three-year funding commitment. SDGs offer a great framework to align your institution's mission and goals to. Many organisations (governments, industry and civil society) share them. Researchers long to achieve something tangible and real. This is a great driver of engagement that should be harnessed.

Look for opportunities to demonstrate convergence and diversity of expertise across STEM, humanities, arts, and social sciences that you can use to understand a problem more broadly from many angles. For instance, understanding ethics and behaviour change is critical for the effective roll-out and societal acceptance of many technologies like AI.

Aim to create an MoU for how you can work together, although remember that implementation is much harder than signing up. MoUs may not always lead to broader Master Collaboration Agreements, covering both programmatic and philanthropic engagements, although they are a starter towards this aim. Good research contracts staff are extremely valuable. They will ensure that compliance and due diligence checks have been undertaken.

Understand and demonstrate mutual benefit and mutual respect

Alliance leaders must assess and map their complementary assets and consider value co-creation. Ask industry for a non-confidential priorities list highlighting their interest areas. Much of this information is available through investor reports that can be searched for by keyword via many bibliometric resources online.

You should demonstrate how you will create added value through an alliance, addressing the 'what's in it for me?' question. You should be able to explain in one sentence to your industry contact how you will be able to achieve more together rather than alone in tackling a particular challenge. This could mean being able to amplify and accelerate efforts to address a particular challenge such as gender equality in an area like computer science, through Master scholarships focused on attracting people from under-represented backgrounds.

Alliance managers should show how they can help academics to grow relationships, provide real benefits to companies and good customer service to both internal and external customers. This means that they do not need to feel they must be in the driving seat of every corporate relationship within the university; however, we recommend they should at least be in the passenger seat to ensure that the driver navigates the road ahead carefully.

Large technology and management consultancies can offer access to their customers across many fields through industry-focused student projects. In the US, such initiatives are known as 'capstone programmes'. Starting relationships with industry through engagement around student projects can help to demonstrate the added value of your talented students addressing problems, whether from industry, clinical or charitable partners. Often companies will use student projects to explore adjacent market areas or new technology areas of interest where they lack expertise and wish to leverage innovative thinking while also scouting for talent. Companies are often flexible around open-sourcing the outputs of such projects.

Whenever you start new engagements with industry partners, aim to achieve relationships that have a growth mindset from the beginning. For example, a successful experience for partners with industry-focused student projects leads to a company offering work placements and then funded PhD research opportunities.

Investment decisions by companies in whether to fund the initiation of a university alliance are based on several key criteria:

- identification of end-user: can we solve a customer problem or issue together through this alliance?

- feasibility of project: how technically and organisationally viable is this initiative or research challenge to be worked on together through this alliance?
- commercial value: what is the likelihood that this alliance will provide a financial gain for the business?
- ROI: what economic and social benefits are expected to result from this alliance? Will this alliance be a brand differentiator?

Potential assets that result from the collaboration should be considered and listed at an early stage. These may include impactful case studies, joint publications, and press releases, proof of concepts and open-source code.

Talent acquisition is a vital driver for university–industry alliances and provides a very effective 'gateway activity' to fostering partnerships. It requires companies to raise their brand awareness on campus

Understand where your institutional strengths are and how they are integrated across the university. For example, an innovative curriculum involving industry projects can give your university a real USP when engaging with industry.

Proactive partner research, selection and approach

Alliance managers need to have a clear pitch, and academics must have a specific ask when speaking to companies. They should coordinate circulating RFPs to relevant academic staff. Set up a notification system internally. Aim to secure 'deep dive' meetings or pitches with senior executives by proactively responding to RFPs.

For collaborative research opportunities, such as offered by government funding bodies, rather than contract research, we recommend finding industry partners who are undertaking high-quality science, evidenced through publications either authored by or sponsored by the company. In the UK, you can search 'UKRI Grants on the Web' to see which companies have co-funded research with government funding bodies and who have a track record of working with academia.

You should seek to find partners with an appropriate critical mass of complementary research facilities, technology, and scale to make an impact on the UN SDGs. Build relationships by sharing thought leadership and strategic thinking about climate change and the SDGs, for example. This is where foresight planning to consider trends for different sectors can be very helpful. Talk to your experts in the university, and do competitor and industry intelligence gathering. 5th generation universities will be highly effective at understanding and acting on trends in society to grow partnerships.

Offer ExecEd in areas of growing interest to an industry audience, for example in quantum computation, or AI/ML. Consider the 'freemium' business model – what resources can be offered for free, or on a pilot/introductory basis at a discount?

Companies are interested in exploitation of research and can often be willing to offer access to testbed environments, for example a construction company offering a building site for testing a novel radar or measurement tool developed by academics. Such offers can create opportunities for collaborations to grow and, as academics demonstrate their capability to industry, it is then easier to secure funding for research and innovation particularly. Universities can also offer experimental testbeds or 'sandbox environments' to industry, such as novel infrastructure for testing a company's products and services on a trial licence for a fixed period on campus. This can deliver both commercial and societal benefit as well as creating opportunities to birth transformational alliances.

Effective business development is proactive rather than reactive. Developing trigger and filter mechanisms can be very helpful for partner selection; however, this relies on pulling data from a range of different sources, such as graduate recruitment and research quality rankings. 'Triggers' are events that may lead to increased interest from companies in forming alliances with universities. These may occur, for instance, when major competitors of companies sign joint MoUs focused on innovation or when a company is facing regulatory change, for example the move towards all cars being electric by 2030 in the UK. 'Filters' could be whether a company recruits significant numbers of graduates from your country, highlighting a need to grow their talent pipeline through working with universities.

We advise collaborating with both business librarians within your institution and specialist prospect researchers (often found within leading university advancement teams). Competitor intelligence through web-based research is also important to learn whether companies already have strategic alliances with partner universities in your region.

Start small and grow trusted relationships

Effective alliances almost always start small and scale. In the US, UC Berkeley started joint research with a large multinational chemical company that led to several joint publications over the next few years. As a result of the demonstrable value that this alliance provided to the company, and because of a 'tipping point' level of trust being built in the relationship, the company made a multi-million-dollar philanthropic capital gift for a new research centre.

Develop simple ideas, proof-of-concept studies, short early feasibility studies and demonstrators so you can have something to show company executives when they visit your campus. Start a potential alliance relationship with roundtable meetings for senior staff to share ideas and different perspectives on problems with their peers from industry. Be transparent in all communications to build mutual understanding. Nurture and strengthen relationships through student projects. Demonstrate patience, flexibility and confidence to overcome early challenges to your alliance. You should seek to understand the different structures, individual roles, language and requirements of organisations.

Industry internships for PhD students will become a feature of 5th generation universities likely to span different continents in alliance with universities between the Global North and Global South to address the UN SDGs. These universities will demonstrate a desire to enable students to see how their research addresses real-world challenges and gain an immersive experience in industry before graduating. Universities and companies involved with PhD internships should ensure these hybrid experiences allow PhD students to gain exposure to senior leaders and influencers. Your PhD students can be highly effective assets in strengthening engagements. This is also the case where postdocs are facilitators within industry-funded CoEs, growing the 'stickiness' of engagement between university and industry partner. Universities can also work with companies to create employee PhD programmes to build their talent pipeline for R&D and innovation.

Adjunct or honorary lecturers from industry, who either give their time for free or work part time as academics, are an increasingly important, although still underutilised, tool for growing partnerships with industry, offering a triple win for university, company and student:

- companies – help to retain talent;
- universities – help to share workload and grow deeper engagement with industry;
- students – help to make lectures more relevant with real-world examples.

Alliance leaders should brief their academics before they pitch to an industry audience using our ASK. method, shown in Figure 3.5, which helps academics who act as start-up CEOs to think like entrepreneurs. This preparation can help your academics to rehearse their approach and take a step closer to understanding the company that they are planning to engage with. Pre-meetings with academics before meeting with industry can help to set a good agenda, orchestrate discussion topics and set mutual goals.

5th generation universities are not interested in passive engagements with industry. Universities will increasingly seek new perspectives on problems by engaging with different sectors and this will open new solutions for society. They wish

Figure 3.5: The ASK method

What is your ASK?

Academics think like a startup

Academics need to think and act like entrepreneurs to develop Transformational Strategic Alliances with industry:

Academic Excellence

- Proactively seek out co-innovation industry partners
- Mutual benefit – answer 'what's in it for me?'

Startup Pitch

- Pitch value and disruptive ideas to potential partners
- Develop a sustainable business model e.g. IP, licensing

Know your audience

- Demonstrate minimum viable product e.g. tabletop kit/software/PoC to achieve significant impact through an active two-way rather than transactional engagement. Passive engagements around joint publications alone, for example, offer limited ROI for both universities and industry.

However, facilitating co-location of joint researchers and students between university and industry offers a greater ROI opportunity for both partners and can help develop trust more effectively. Students are the glue in between university academics and researchers from companies. Internships can help to facilitate deeper relationships that may grow into research collaborations. Likewise, competitions and hackathons are very popular with students and can also help to deepen trusted relationships.

Embed an entrepreneurial alliance culture that values knowledge exchange brokers

Alliance managers in universities are value creators, spanning the boundary between the academic world that can sometimes look very closed to the outside world. They initiate and orchestrate mutually beneficial relationships between organisations with different cultures.

Business development is one core skill of strategic alliance managers. They promote research partnerships, technology solutions or business services. They have an armoury of corporate intelligence, CRM and tools for planning alliances. They have mapped complementary assets beyond finance that corporates can combine with the university for mutual benefit. They always seek to maximise the contributions and impact of academics' presentations and visits from industry to academic labs through careful preparation and briefing. In this way, they proactively add value to academics' and researchers' engagement with industry.

They can influence and engage through strong communication and interpersonal skills. They understand the elements of negotiation and deal creation. They can sense where there may be stormy waters ahead for relationships by pre-empting problems so they can be resolved early. They are transparent and able to speak up and flag potential problems that need addressing in advance. People 'buy' from people – personal relationships are at the heart of strong alliance-building. Innovation happens through people who are 'on the same page' within networks of trust.

Create a structured and agile customer 'journey' to make a blended approach to collaboration easier

Building the right structure and internal processes for partnerships is very important. This requires flexibility and the ability to find timelines that work for both parties in terms of deliverables. It is important to agree on the route or pathway to impact, whether through partnership and engagement activity in research, teaching or innovation.

Our contractual engagement model (Figure 1.13) highlights the importance of simplicity in engagement, starting with 'Identification', then 'Discovery', before 'Alignment'. This requires academics and alliance leaders not getting too technical in early-stage discussions. Bringing the right experts together at the alignment or 'roundtable' stage is important, so there is a good conversation that will add value to both sides. These workshops should seek to stretch the understanding of the problem that partners are looking to tackle by bringing together academics from a range of disciplinary backgrounds. In our experience, industry really appreciates the breadth of disciplinary insight brought to bear on problems from universities.

Agility in your contracting process can lead to higher responsiveness and faster contracting overall. In doing this, your objective should always be to create an improved customer 'journey' by being an easier university to collaborate with. This requires the right legal contracting support who understand 'blended' research-innovation collaborative models and process/workflow automation.

Master collaboration agreements are increasingly used by corporations looking to form alliances with universities to cover their multifaceted engagements across research, innovation, and philanthropy, offering greater flexibility and agility in how they can progress collaborations. These may include projects funded both through donations and directly sponsored research with different IP terms. University research contracts teams are historically focused on traditional government-funded research grants rather than more innovation-focused agreements. Corporate funding cycles often mean that, at the end of each quarter and financial year, underspends in budgets need to be utilised within units such as the university relations or R&D teams, or they will be lost. If universities have already signed a master collaboration agreement with a corporate, it is much easier to access such funds in an agile way throughout the year. Once signed, they require effective programme and relationship management to be in place to ensure success.

Measure the shared value, impact and societal benefit your alliance is creating

There are many ways to capture and record the value that you create through your engagement activity and how that impacts the research, teaching and innovation in your institution. Make use of the UN SDG Engagement Canvas in Table 2.7. The Balanced Scorecard tool (see Figure 3.6) can also be useful in setting the metrics used to measure progress towards shared objectives at regular intervals. We recommend this is done at least quarterly. There should be designated leads within each partner for gathering data on these metrics. This could include both quantitative information, for example delivering to time and budget on the development of a working prototype, and qualitative information, for example about quality of dialogue between parties.

Foster co-location

Innovation scholars and policy experts have advocated the importance of co-location for accelerating the growth of strong alliances, providing shared space for serendipitous exchanges to take place. Human beings are social creatures and trust-forming is dependent on frequent contact. Will digital collaboration technologies make face-to-face, in-person contact less important in future for trust-building and strengthening alliances? We believe that the future of collaboration will be blended multi-sector communication and interaction.

Post-pandemic collaborative research environments will allow industry and academia to work in close proximity on advancing research and development for social benefit. These spaces will be underpinned by excellent infrastructure supporting seamless digital collaboration technologies enabling a wider range of partners globally, including from the Global South, to collaborate across sectors, as never before.

Create engaging testbeds and demonstrators for industry visitors

Universities are keen to understand real-life problems from industry. By creating engaging testbeds, demonstrators or 'living labs' where technology PoCs arising from applied research can be demonstrated, you can host groups from industry and demonstrate your capabilities (Figure 3.4). Industry is also keen to provide testbeds and test sites for demonstrators of technology from universities: for example, a construction firm may be happy to have a novel system for the construction sector on their building site. Within the humanities, policy labs can also be developed. Good practice on campus related to the SDGs, for example, zero-carbon buildings, should be shown to industry.

Ensure strong, open and regular communications both internally and externally

How you communicate and how frequently you communicate, whether via email, remote via conference call or in person, is very important. It is also essential to take into account cultural factors to ensure effective communications. For example, Japanese companies can take a very cautious, step by step approach, which is also hierarchical, top-down. The Japanese have a word for this part of their business culture, 'Nemawashi', which translates 'turning the roots' or 'laying the groundwork'.[10]

Mapping, retaining and boosting partnerships

The Pareto principle, or 80/20 rule, states that 80 per cent of your income and engagement from corporates will come from

20 per cent of the companies that you work with. We have found this to be the case in our own experience. Once the university at either central, faculty or department level have analysed which 20 per cent of companies provide most of your corporate income, they should focus their strategy on retaining and boosting their engagement with these companies. This involves profiling or segmenting the companies you have alliances with. It is important to ensure that those companies align with your values and institutional mission as you seek to have a greater focus on addressing societal challenges like the UN SDGS.

Reaching out through your alumni network

Once you have completed intelligence gathering on potential collaborators and mapped out your institution's expertise and capabilities (Chapter 2), how should you reach out to new contacts who you would like to connect with to discuss partnership opportunities? A good place to start is through your alumni network. Your alumni are valuable assets as door-openers and advocates as they have experienced the value of your university first-hand as students themselves and are often keen to assist growing partnerships. This is particularly the case if you can find a senior or 'C-level' alumnus who can act as an Executive Champion in a company in a peer-to-peer governance structure.

When you approach alumni, you should write with authenticity and keep messaging short and to the point. This is also true for all email communications with managers and senior executives from industry. You should frequently reflect on, learn from, and iterate how you communicate via email as well as during online or in-person meetings with industry, and ask yourself how you can do better.

Here is an example of an email or calendar invitation to set up a Discovery Workshop session, following an introductory call with an alumnus:

> Dear NAME – thanks for your email and interest in participating in a Discovery session. We would normally schedule about 1.5 hours for this to work

out specific areas for our alliance to focus on. Please find hereafter an indicative agenda for your perusal:

- Introductions – 5 mins
- Overview of company – 15 mins
- Overview of university and alliance team focus areas – 15 mins
- Overview of specific activities/programmes of most relevance – 15 mins
- Alliance opportunities related to most relevant collaboration area identified – 30 mins
- Next steps & AOB – 10 mins

Workflow automation, customer relationship management systems and data visualisation

5th generation universities embrace digital transformation by utilising workflow automation and implementing an effective CRM system across their institutions. CRM systems linked and integrated to email, forms, canvases, strategy documents and other document management systems can be very powerful tools for alliance management. Workflow automation is becoming increasingly important for universities in an era of digital transformation. When implemented well, this can offer huge efficiency savings.

Data visualisation tools offer great graphical insights into data held in CRM systems on industry partnerships: for example, who your most important customers are in terms of both incomes received and the companies' wider non-cash contributions to the university. However, data visualisation can also be used for mapping institutional activity more broadly related to the UN SDGs, whether through research, teaching or KE.

Universities must innovate both their products and services as well as their administrative processes. As well as the entrepreneurial academic, universities also need *intra*preneurial (within organisation) professional service managers and leaders (see Table 2.4). Process workflow automation will become increasingly important for next generation universities. As student projects with industry partners scale, for example, there is a huge need for rapid contracting via products such as e-signature, cloud-based software for automated compliance processes with minimum human intervention. Universities that embrace this will gain a competitive advantage and will find greater opportunities to improve efficiency and engagement with industry partners.

Developing an effective system of alliance partner relationship management is a key success factor. Trialling the implementation of a CRM through a pilot or PoC within one faculty with the greatest corporate engagement is an effective way to demonstrate the usefulness of such systems and gain internal champions before a wider roll-out. We recommend setting up a cross-institutional project team to source requirements for a CRM through an in-depth discovery phase before delivery and implementation.

It is important not to rush into implementing a CRM by purchasing off-the-shelf systems without having the necessary institutional support and buy-in. CRMs within universities are more common among advancement and fundraising teams rather than wider external corporate engagement teams. They have been developed to keep track of engagements with individual philanthropic donors, from both alumni and non-alumni. It is vital that this data is integrated and shared effectively with knowledge exchange and external engagement teams in other university business units. This requires strong governance from senior leadership to make such cooperation happen across the university.

CRMs must be used proactively and, while they are never likely to capture every interaction with industry in a large university, they can help to effectively manage engagement with your most important industry alliance partners, providing a better client experience. CRMs must be more than a data repository and deliver corporate intelligence, trend information and actionable insights that can boost your marketing, business development and KE efforts.

Tool – Balanced Scorecard for keep track of Key Performance Indicators

In this chapter, we discussed the importance of mutually agreeing metrics with your alliance partner during the 'norming and performing' stage of alliance formation (Table 3.1). The

Balanced Scorecard (Figure 3.6) can be used to measure these metrics throughout the duration of your alliance at quarterly management meetings, to ensure that your alliance remains on track and maintains buy-in from both sides.

The Scorecard is 'balanced' because it takes account of four critical areas of outputs, outcomes and impact arising from the ongoing alliance activity, and measures progress towards achieving shared objectives. The metrics must be discussed and selected together with your industry partner and there must be a balanced number of metrics in each quadrant related to ways of measuring success that are important for both the university and the corporate.

5th generation universities will have an integrated approach to metrics, recognising the overlapping benefits and added value of alliances related to research, teaching and KE. What metrics are important to measure? Possible success measures for both sides within alliances are shown in Table 3.3.

Companies will often evaluate how quickly collaborative projects with universities can move from initial discussion to deployment of 'products' that deliver commercial return. Increasingly they want to see a shorter time to achieve impact at scale and so in certain areas of fast-moving technology we are likely to see a reduced appetite for funding PhDs and more

Figure 3.6: An example of the four quadrants of a Balanced Scorecard

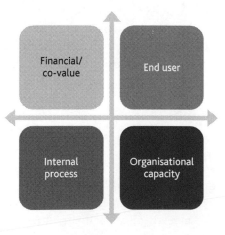

Table 3.3: The different Key Performance Indicators for universities and industry to measure in their alliances

University KPIs	Industry KPIs
#Student internships/graduate jobs	#New hires
#Publications	#Patents
#Impact case studies/positive press releases	#Media mentions/PR
Raised brand awareness/reputation	Raised brand awareness/reputation
Success in government assessment, for example UK's REF, TEF, KEF or equivalent	#New products launched
#Licences from industry	Return on Investment (ROI)
Philanthropic income	#New client relationships leveraged through university ecosystem
Consultancy income	#Positive Senior Leadership Team (SLT) mentions
#Executive visits and level of peer-to-peer engagement	#Student-to-employee conversions
Quality of dialogue and level of trust	Quality of dialogue and level of trust
#Projects funded related to the UN SDGs	#Projects funded related to the UN SDGs
Quality of innovation ecosystem leveraged	Quality of innovation ecosystem leveraged

Note: # indicates 'number of'.

interest in shorter-term innovation projects involving student start-ups and academic spinouts.

Case study: A longstanding transformational strategic alliance between a leading university and a large, multinational corporate

This case study is based on a 30+-year transformational strategic alliance between a global top 10 university in the UK (named as 'the University' throughout this case study), and a multinational, world-leading tech company headquartered in the US (named as 'the Corporate' throughout).

A strong relationship between the University and the Corporate began over 30 years ago during the birth of the internet and email. The relationship developed between senior Computer Science academics from the University and technical staff from the Corporate. Delivering societal benefit was at the core of the engagement from the very beginning, with a strong focus on innovation and improving global communications infrastructure. Commercialisation of co-created, novel products and solutions was also very important for the Corporate.

The relationship expanded to cover all areas of the University's mission – research, teaching and KE – and became a strategic alliance (see Figure 3.7). Today, the alliance provides a blueprint for many other universities and corporates on a global basis. It has achieved a clear win–win for both organisations and enabled them achieve more together than they could do independently. Some of the joint programmes worth mentioning are highlighted.

Figure 3.7: Multi-faceted engagement delivered through a 30+ year transformational strategic alliance between a leading university and multinational technology corporate

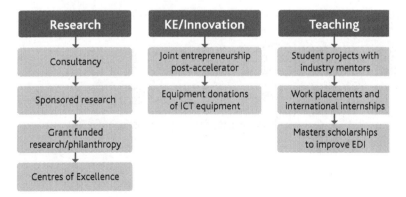

An international internship programme

This programme lasted seven years and involved almost a hundred penultimate-year undergraduate and Master students from multiple academic disciplines including Computer Science, Electronic and Electrical Engineering (EEE) and Management, spending a year in Silicon Valley as part of their degree on a work-based placement. At least a third of these students gained employment in the Corporate after graduating. The students became great ambassadors within the Corporate for the University and helped to strengthen and expand the alliance into new areas. As connections grew between the University's academics and the Corporate, research sponsorship through donation from the Corporate's philanthropic foundation as well as directly funded sponsored research soon started to flow.

The secret of the programme's success was having a very senior alumnus who was an Executive Champion in the Corporate. Regular reporting and checking in on students and their managers by the University, as well as annual campus visits by senior management from the Corporate, were also important factors to improve communications and build trust.

It is also worth noting the importance of flexibility, alliance management, customer service and an innovative approach on the part of the University, which created new degree programmes and structures that would align with the Corporate's talent acquisition needs and students' interests in pursuing a transformational work-based learning opportunity.

Centres of Excellence

The Corporate became a founding sponsor of several CoEs within the University related to emerging and strategic technology areas of interest. Each CoE enabled a deeper interaction between University and Corporate staff and helped to grow levels of trust. For the Corporate, the CoE model helped to raise the brand awareness and recognition nationally (particularly with government) and internationally as innovation leaders. For the University, the CoE model helped to demonstrate impact through KE.

Post-accelerator/Innovation Centre

There are a myriad of innovation centres (pre- and post-accelerators) in the University both for students who own the IPR of their research projects and the staff spinouts. As part of this overarching model, the Corporate co-funded the set-up of a post-accelerator within the city region of the University. This boosted economic development through job creation, attracting significant venture capital and creating a growing innovation ecosystem. As part of the Corporate's commitment to the post-accelerator, it made a significant donation of equipment to improve facilities within the Innovation Centre. The post-accelerator hosted regular and spontaneous visits from the C-level executive leadership team of the Corporate and University.

Masters scholarships

The Corporate wished to support Master-level scholarships targeting students from under-represented backgrounds in line with their strong EDI values, shared with the University. This significant strategic corporate philanthropy highlights how the alliance has now become transformational, targeting together SDG 4 (quality education), SDG 5 (gender equality), SDG 8 (good jobs and economic growth), SDG 9 (innovation and infrastructure) and SDG 17 (partnerships for the goals).

Summary

This alliance could be described as a triple win for the University, the Corporate and wider society through the creation of new opportunities, employment, and scholarships for students from under-represented backgrounds. The Corporate draws on the complementary expertise and resources of the University, and vice versa. The Corporate continues to enhance their global reputation and competitive edge through this alliance and creates new networks and opportunities for high-impact research for the University.

Lessons learned

- Industry and academia both have different motivations for partnership development, and it is important to find alignment of vision, mission and values for any collaborative project to be successful.

- 5th generation universities will adopt a data-centric approach to acquiring internal intelligence on university research strengths, and industry intelligence gathering by utilising many new bibliometric tools and having a dedicated alliance team.
- The Balanced Scorecard tool can be useful in setting the metrics used to measure progress towards shared objectives at regular intervals. We recommend this is done at least quarterly.
- Within knowledge-based economies and societies, university–industry alliances and an expanded concept of multi-sector helix combinations are important for understanding the non-linear and 'messy' process of innovation.
- Remember that famous quote from Thomas A. Edison: 'Vision without execution is hallucination.' Obviously, it is always great to have vision. It is all fine and good to know your why, but if you cannot execute it, then that is no value whatsoever.
- Every strategic alliance team and professional should have their own VSEM. This enables you to ensure your institutional vision for building partnerships with industry is strategically aligned internally and operationalised effectively.
- From a university's standpoint, always remember to answer the "What's in it for me?" question from industry. Prepare a high-level menu of what kind of products and services (institutional assets) you are willing to offer. The same way of thinking applies the other way around as well. It is now increasingly expected that the industry should also know what they can genuinely offer to academia in exchange.
- 5th generation universities will embrace the Ten Principles, illustrated in Figure 3.4, for building strong alliances to address the UN SDGs that are now at the top of every corporate's business agenda.
- Use the Pareto principle, or 80/20 rule, in your engagements to concentrate your efforts on your most important industry partners.
- Make use of a CRM system to map alliances and university–industry interactions. This is key to ensure institutional alignment and monitoring, and to provide excellent customer service to your trusted and valuable partners. CRM systems linked and integrated to email, forms, canvases, strategy documents and other document management systems can be

very powerful, especially through process workflow automation that is now increasingly important for universities in an era of digital transformation. When implemented well, they can offer huge efficiency savings.

4

Leading and executing sustainable relationships

Perhaps one day they will add about you as their leader,
"And you made a difference." That is the true reward
of Leadership.

John Eric Adair, leadership theorist,
from his book *Develop Your Leadership Skills*[1]

How do both universities and corporates build effective strategic alliance functionality in their organisations so they can lead and execute long-lasting relationships to achieve positive change in society? In this chapter we offer advice on both leadership strategy and execution, as a strategy is only of value when it is implemented effectively. A poor strategy well implemented is better than a good strategy poorly executed.

We can all exercise leadership, in our families, in our work environments and in wider society, through our actions and attitudes. There are several clear differences between leaders and managers, and we explain how good leadership is essential for transformational strategic alliances.

We will explore how 5th generation universities will take an active role in leading alliances. They will develop clearly defined, robust processes for governing their external engagement. They will effectively facilitate a transformational approach to strategic alliances both within global academia as well as outside of higher education, through operationalising effective collaboration mechanisms.

Alliance design and governance

According to Ankrah and Al Tabbaa (2015),[2] there has been little scholarly work on the drivers and mechanisms of alliances. In our experience, university–industry relationships are never fully integrated in a single office as they are multidimensional. Instead of a single office, 5th generation universities have clear governance and alignment of policies concerning the management and leadership of university–industry alliances. Clear communication of these policies will ensure that distributed teams across the layers of universities understand each other's role. How will you know what success looks like in your university's alliance design and governance? It is when, as an alliance leader, you can co-create value with agility and efficacy, building critical mass internally while constantly maintaining a high level of energy externally propelling your alliance activity.

Are you thinking 5th generationally?

Key questions for university leaders to gauge their appetite for building a 5th generation university that enables transformational alliances are as follows:

- What benefit can your alumni network provide? Are they seen as predominantly advocates and influencers, or mainly a source of cash for years after graduating?
- How are you structuring your functionality for building strong external relationships with corporates? What are the benefits of centralisation versus decentralisation?
- Why should automating your contractual framework process and embracing digital transformation help your university to achieve its institutional mission?
- How are you exercising leadership skills to ensure your most important industry relationships can be strengthened?
- In what ways do recognition and reward structures encourage your academics and professional services staff to engage effectively with industry?

- What are the means to measure the societal benefit arising from your university's engagement with industry?
- How effectively are you leveraging large intergovernmental organisations to gain visibility of your university's research, teaching and innovation to an industry audience?

5th generation universities will have a senior leadership team who understand that innovation is about executing sustainable relationships that lead to positive change for the world. They are a hot bed for fresh thinking that delivers action in terms of doing new, relevant and important things for the 'common good'. This understanding of innovation recognises that building alliances is not for the sake of alliances, but to make things happen for societal benefit and positive change.

Economics Professor Theodore Levitt's insight about innovation is just as relevant for leaders of universities as for business: "Creativity thinks up new things. Innovation does new things. The difference speaks for itself. Yet the fluent advisers to business seldom make the distinction. They tend to rate ideas more by their novelty than by their practicality."[3]

When thinking about solutions to the UN SDGs, 5th generation universities will recognise that they need to find practical solutions for people (Table 1.5). These solutions do not necessarily always have to be the most technologically advanced. This insight comes from the appropriate technology movement. To paraphrase the title of the famous collection of essays published in 1973 by E.F. Schumacher that helped to initiate this movement – small is often beautiful.[4]

Building on such an understanding of international development and humanitarianism, 5th generation universities will seek to bring multidisciplinary expertise from the social sciences and humanities as well as STEM to address complex challenges through both incremental and disruptive innovation. While they recognise that discovering and supporting disruptive innovators is vital due to the urgent challenges facing the world, all innovation across disciplines towards the UN SDGs is valued, respected and celebrated.

Internal restructuring to improve efficiency of alliance activity

How do you know when it may be necessary to restructure to increase the efficiency and effectiveness of your alliance activity? What is the innovation support infrastructure required to achieve Minimum Viable Partnerships (MVPs), from which transformational strategic alliances can emerge? We argue that 5th generation universities will have learned to innovate in their alliance models, by developing a holistic and structured approach to their engagement with industry, NGOs and government. They also have streamlined business processes through workflow automation that has significantly reduced the timescales for research contracting, for example. Finally, they have also improved their coordination between all the external-facing parts of their institutions, in alignment with their vision and academic mission, that includes a strong focus on achieving the UN SDGs (Table 1.5).

Tiering up and affiliate programmes

Tiering your alliances with industry is a structured portfolio approach that is primarily for internal resource management whereas affiliate programmes involve offering paid-for tiered alliance opportunities externally with associated benefits. Tiering your alliances by level of income, for example, is an effective way to ensure that you focus your time and effort on delighting your most important customers. This is in line with the Pareto principle, also known as the 80/20 rule (as discussed in Chapter 3), where 20 per cent of your customers account for 80 per cent of your income. We suggest you tier your alliances based on a company's strategic relevance towards achieving the UN SDGs. This assumes that 80 per cent of your impact will come from the 20 per cent most engaged of your industry partners.

Tiering can help to improve internal coordination and visibility of your most important alliances and to ensure that conversations with large companies, across different departments and academics, are not contradictory. It can also improve your internal resource allocation and ensure that you are able to provide a certain level of service to clients.

Many leading universities have set up affiliate programmes to facilitate corporate engagement, and used effectively, with the right resources, such programmes can be very productive.

Dealing with internal politics and barriers

In 2019, an international study produced the first map of the underground social network of roots, fungi and bacteria that enable trees and plants to communicate with each other in a symbiotic manner for mutual benefit. This incredible network has become known as the 'wood wide web' and researchers believe it is important for limiting climate change.[5] Likewise, the social networks created through multi-sector partnership and alliance activity become symbiotic and actors within the network can provide an early warning system through effective communications with partners when threatened with internal and external barriers to positive change.

Your personal connections within your institution at all levels are vital for helping you to face difficult periods of internal politics and challenges in your institution's relationship with companies. How effectively are you able to orchestrate different stakeholders to 'win friends and influence people' internally to achieve change? This leadership skill of handling organisational change wisely is to create a sense of co-ownership, a mentality of 'we are here to help ensure that this alliance is a success for both parties'.

Alliance leaders often consider the question, 'Who are the detractors and distractors in this alliance journey?' Some people will deliberately seek to distract your alliance and derail it. Others will seek to detract, criticise, and seek to scale back your mutually agreed ambitions. Your job is to be a wise steward of the relationship between your university and industry, holding the door open for others within your institution to add value, for mutual and societal benefit. To achieve this, you will need to find a like-minded, respected and well-connected individual within your partner organisation. This will help to develop a sense of co-ownership in ensuring the health of your alliance remains strong and can withstand any storm.

We have found that using internal briefings and vision papers can help to improve communication and secure wider executive support internally. This is not a delivery or execution plan but a short summary to get everyone around the same objectives for the alliance and typically covers the following:

- background to the alliance;
- purpose or objective of the alliance;
- vision of the alliance and how this relates to your wider university vision;
- expected outputs or key results offering value to the university and society;
- next steps;
- timelines for next 12 months.

Key barriers to developing KE and alliance activity within universities, in our experience and often identified in surveys of senior KE leaders, include:

- the culture among academics of prioritising publications in high-quality journals;
- competing/conflicting demands on academics' time;
- internal structures and bureaucracy;
- staff incentives for KE and external engagement activity;
- a very low-risk appetite for innovation in engagement activity with industry particularly.

5th generation universities will learn how to grow staff enthusiasm for KE and an organisational willingness to engage externally by no longer focusing on being the best *in* the world, but rather the best *for* the world. They will have both academic and professional services promotion processes that support and reward KE activity that contributes to successful, transformational strategic alliances delivering real value to the university.

These future universities will have a leadership that tell stories endorsing successful alliances, so staff become aware of the priority of building partnerships for positive change in which KE and engagement are no longer 'third mission' but just part of the core mission. They will create a culture of multi-sector alliances with industry as being a normal part of academic life. This is about changing the discourse around the purpose of universities so that KE and cross-sector strategic alliances more broadly are seen as being vital for underpinning the future of the role of universities in society.

Traditional, 3rd and 4th generation universities prioritise securing research funding and publications in the most prestigious, 'high-impact' journals as the main criteria for academic career progression. They rarely have clear promotion processes for their professional services staff, including for alliance leaders and managers. 5th generation universities have a more inclusive approach to their promotion processes. For academic staff, they assess research publications and grant funding, and for all staff, they recognise and reward valorisation activity that leads to initiating, leading and executing sustainable and transformational strategic alliances and KE. Pioneering universities of the future will have reward structures focused on assessing benefits realisation and contribution towards achieving institutional mission objectives through collaboration. In this sense, such universities will be more 'purpose driven' than ever before towards achieving societal benefit and rediscovering their role as a force for positive change in the world.

Pivoting through partnership and innovation: understanding market pull and technology push

The recent pandemic has created new opportunities as well as challenges for higher education. Many companies are looking for partnering to solve new problems, both nationally and globally. How can you build, strengthen and expand strategic multi-sector alliances in your institution for mutual and societal benefit?

5th generation universities will ask, 'Who are the early adopters of new technologies?' They will consider which companies are more likely to respond to market pull rather than technology push. For example, some leading technology companies with research labs at the frontier of science are early adopters of new technologies who may have a technology roadmap of over 10 years ahead (technology push), and are happy for academia to approach them proactively with collaborative research ideas.

Other companies post RFPs that give a great idea of they are interested in, and are looking for from universities, in terms of new technologies. This is a market-pull and challenge-led approach that responds to the needs of the market. RFPs are low cost but can be used to broaden a company's innovation and partnership funnel and accelerate their understanding of which academics and universities are working in relevant areas. Responding to RFPs can lead to either grant-funded (open-source) research or sponsored research funding for more commercially focused research.

Many companies are surprisingly open about their research and innovation strategy and objectives. It often makes good business sense to crowdsource innovation with universities. There is an increasing trend towards more 'open innovation' calls among leading companies. We recommend finding partners who value open innovation, where researchers can initiate proposals as well as respond to specific business challenges outlined in an RFP.

The best surfers have learned to recognise that every wave is different, and they use their skills gained from practice and experience to keep riding waves, even when faced with difficult conditions. Similarly, alliance leaders need to become adept at riding and adapting to the challenges of different waves of collaboration. While this is inherently risky, with experience and reflection, alliance leadership becomes easier through practice, occasionally making mistakes, and learning quickly from those mistakes to improve in future. 5th generation universities will support such a learning culture for innovation.

Alongside aligned vision, mission and priorities, companies are looking for academics who understand and are adaptable to different industry funding models such as donation or sponsored research and who are interested in validation of their value proposition by an industry partner. They require streamlined processes around contracting and effective coordination to navigate the maze of university administration and often look for a history of successful collaborations with other industry partners, for example evidenced by joint publications.

We have found that if companies will not share their exact problems, they are often more willing to share their objectives for their business.

How long should an alliance last?

You should always seek to build long-term alliances; however, these do not always last forever. Alliance leaders need to learn to be able to finish well: to end and scale down alliances when necessary. It is a good rule of thumb to think up to five years ahead for your alliances, while building in a review after three years, for example, when setting up Strategic Research Centres of Excellence. Building in review points, or 'go/no-go' gates, is sensible to provide agreed academic and corporate reflection times on the progress of the alliance. This is wise from a risk management perspective.

As mentioned earlier, it is also important to capture institutional learnings from each of your alliance experiences, both from those in senior leadership as well as those in middle management involved in the day-to-day operational side of relationship building with companies. This ensures that tacit knowledge is not lost, for example, if a particular academic or alliance manager with a good company relationship should move on from your institution.

When may it be necessary for an alliance to come to an end? You may decide together that the collaboration needs to be stopped due to changing organisational priorities or lack of institutional support internally. Alternatively, you may decide together to pivot the alliance, by taking a different approach. While designing alliances to last and to deliver is important, it is also necessary to be able to adapt your alliance building when required. This could be triggered by changes in your wider innovation ecosystem, a loss of key personnel, geopolitical issues, or a host of other reasons.

Which sectors are most open to innovation?

Tom Winstanley, Chief Technology Officer and Head of New Ventures of NTT DATA UK, shares his insight on innovation in an interesting blog post as follows:

> Innovation used to be something that an organisation did to tick a box. Often, to the great detriment of its chances of success, it was done on the periphery of

the organisation. Thankfully, this is no longer the case. Today, innovation is increasingly a holistic endeavour, with leaders championing collaboration not only within the business, but across and between multiple organisations and industries.[6]

Consortia of organisations from across industries will increasingly come together with intergovernmental organisations to form pre-competitive networks seeking to engage with academia. There has been a trend in the West for pre-competitive R&D consortia, where competitors join forces to keep track of technology developments more effectively. Professional business associations and standards bodies are often a source of information about these.

5th generation universities need to know which sectors are most open to innovation, both within and outside their regions. What is the distinctive flavour or specialism of innovation for your region? Universities should work with their local and regional authorities to shape the 'smart specialisation strategy' in their areas. What are your local drivers for innovation? If your university is in a rural area, this could be to retain talent within your region rather than losing talent to urban areas or overseas.

The pandemic, combined with a growth in remote working, has led to an exodus of many talented workers, within the Global North particularly, to rural areas. This provides a new opportunity for talent acquisition for universities in rural areas. Next, you need to consider what will be your focus area for most of your university–industry interactions and how you can optimise these to ensure that you become the number one partner of choice.

In seeking to collaborate with a multinational insurance company, we read through investor reports and noticed that the company was growing through acquisition of other established brands. We realised that this was a trigger for seeking to gain good PR in the region. We knew they were interested in AI/advanced data analytics and data science – all areas of research strength in our institution.

They were a company of significant scale with money to invest in partnership activity, including corporate philanthropy. As a growing company, they were also keen to attract talent and so we spoke about hackathons and student project opportunities.

Insurance is relevant to multiple industry verticals, so is often a good sector to see new trends, for example drone insurance. The company had a strong brand, and sustainability was clearly an important brand value, hence we expected strong interest in an SDG-focused alliance and were proved to be right. We finished our Discovery Workshop with the promise of a decarbonisation report, which we emailed within the next day in a follow-up email to the company.

Brand awareness and due diligence

How can you ensure you have strong due diligence processes in place so that you choose your partners wisely and do not compromise your brand values through poor brand association? Talking about branding is not giving in to the forces of a more marketised higher education; rather, it is about ensuring that your institution is known for what you most value. It is about ensuring that your identity as described in your mission, vision and values is visible in a world craving for attention. It can enable you to attract the partners you need to make the greatest impact on achieving your academic mission.

Your brand is your institutional identity as perceived both within the organisation and by the outside world, and this perception should be aligned and consistent. In other words, if you believe internally within your organisation that your institution is excellent at finding solutions towards the UN SDGs, the world must also know this and see the evidence of this in all you do.

Think global, act local

So, what are the key things universities can do to tackle the SDGs? Think global, act local – by working in transformational strategic alliances between civil society, community groups, local authorities and local companies on relevant localised research and innovation that will address global challenges.

Creating local impact is just as important as global. Many local government bodies, in the UK and other countries that have declared a climate emergency, are seeking to address climate challenges at the local level, including to achieve their own net zero targets. The Net Zero Innovation Programme (NZIP) aims to bring together researchers and local authorities to define and co-create challenges and set up projects to start to address climate challenges.[7] Such funded programmes provide great opportunities for KE, evidence-based policy-making and practical local delivery of projects for positive change.

Example projects could include decarbonising local transport or improving air quality around schools. How can you integrate the SDGs into your campus life and practices, as well as your operations and outreach? This could include carbon footprint mapping or calculator tools, providing training to staff and students about reducing their food waste.

'Public engagement', also known as 'community engagement', is more vital than ever for the future of higher education. 5th generation universities will recognise that they have a moral responsibility to contribute positively to society through their public engagement and have much to gain in return. The grassroots activism of the Black Lives Matter (BLM) movement and the international decolonising agenda have led to universities starting to think more about racial justice and decolonisation. How can this thinking translate into more inclusive engagement, both offline in local communities as well as online, reducing inequalities and boosting EDI initiatives (SDG 10)? Increasingly, research funders, whether from government or industry, will expect universities to support public engagement, and evidence suggests that public engagement is critical to a healthy university.[8]

We value the approach to public engagement known as 'co-production', where alliances deliver equality of benefits for all parties. This trend involves value-based engagement and citizen science that respects our shared humanity and treats all people with dignity regardless of their background. The Co-Production Collective is a diverse, international, and open community that works with mainly public and voluntary sector organisations, including universities, charities, hospitals, housing associations and community groups.[9]

5th generation universities will harness novel approaches to co-production and involve a greater diversity of voices, including from industry, to facilitate transformational research, teaching, innovation, and programme delivery with measurable positive impact on their local communities. This will be especially among those who have been historically under-represented and excluded from influencing research directions. Quintuple helix alliances in 5th generation universities will enable a far greater range of viewpoints to be expressed as there is a greater focus on 'team science', where the team is likely to include representatives from the world's poorest and marginalised.

5th generation universities have reconsidered their role in their local communities and the world. They have reorientated, reformed where necessary, and integrated their research, education and innovation activities, their university curriculums and culture around the UN SDGs. This is reflected in their mission and strategy. As a global public good, they have a social responsibility and an important social justice role to play. They hire people from diverse backgrounds and are highly collaborative, both internally and externally. They support fellowships and activities for under-represented groups. They promote equitable access to new innovations that address grand challenges facing the world and engage with diverse communities locally and globally to tackle problems collaboratively. They foster a collaborative, flexible and transformative culture rather than a competitive, transactional culture. They seek a more equitable and inclusive future for the world.

Practically, this means that 5th generation universities will have proactively developed robust, clearly defined engagement processes, to build trust and help partners, for example, other universities in the Global South, to secure funding from government, industry, or philanthropic foundations to address global challenges collaboratively. This requires alliance leaders among the partners to do the following:

- to have laser-like alignment of objectives, priorities, needs, expectations (key results) and milestones;
- to clarify partner roles, governance structures and the unique value proposition and capabilities/assets that each partner brings to the alliance;
- to assess capacity for risk and how to mitigate this so that responsible innovation is not hindered as it is within agreed boundaries;

- to encourage strong communication and intra-organisational story telling about the transformational value of cross-sector collaboration to bring about positive change;
- to demonstrate strong relationship-building skills and a humble, servant-leadership approach that helps to foster trust among all staff involved in the partnership and to steer partnerships away from obstacles;
- to appoint staff with project management and workflow automation experience to assist in keeping the project on track in terms of timescales and deliverables;
- to record benefits realised and the diverse forms of impact delivered through the alliance, both internally and externally;
- to pivot where necessary so that the alliance can adapt to change – this flexibility is essential and must be present alongside the necessary focus on execution of mutually agreed objectives for the alliance.

Building collective will internally and externally

To solve the complex, wicked problems we face, 5th generation universities will adopt a highly multidisciplinary approach within their institutions. Universities have experts from all disciplines, although often they do not collaborate for a variety of reasons, including national funding structures providing few incentives, rivalry, egos, and poor organisation. This must change.

Universities with vision can build collective will internally and externally to act in partnership to solve important challenges. Transformational strategic alliances, the defining feature of the 5th generation university, can help to scale and drive greater positive change than ever before by drawing on powerful levers of influence from across sectors (see Figure 4.1; the quintuple helix includes ecological factors, or the 'Environment', and can be seen in Figure 1.2).

Building collective will must be led from the top of institutions, and this will also require training to be provided on the benefits of building alliances for positive change. It will likely involve ensuring that your research contracting team gain experience of blended research and innovation contracts, and that your institution has a clear governance process in place to manage

Figure 4.1: Levers of influence for transformation between different sectors

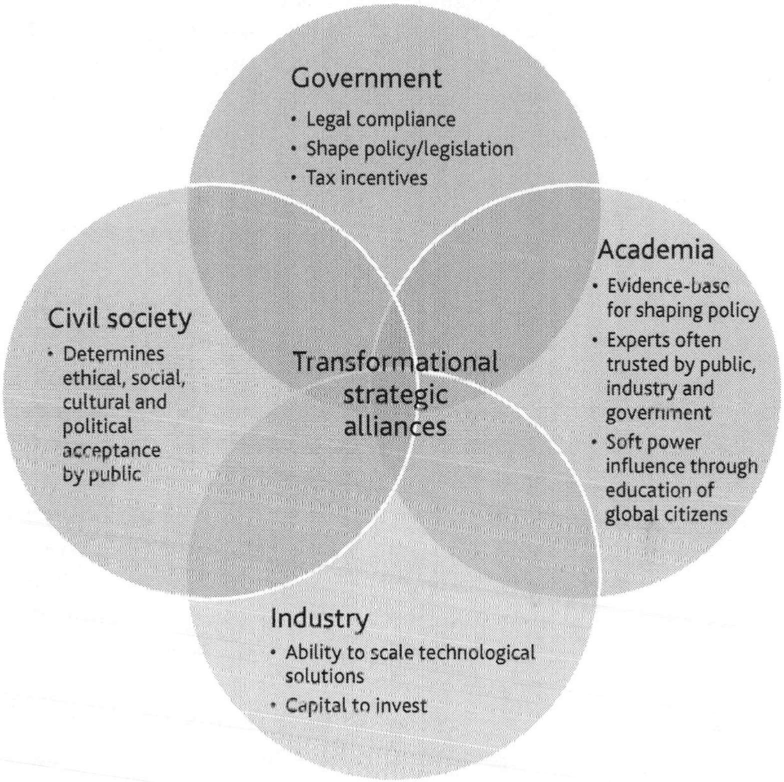

Government
- Legal compliance
- Shape policy/legislation
- Tax incentives

Academia
- Evidence-base for shaping policy
- Experts often trusted by public, industry and government
- Soft power influence through education of global citizens

Civil society
- Determines ethical, social, cultural and political acceptance by public

Transformational strategic alliances

Industry
- Ability to scale technological solutions
- Capital to invest

the agile sign-off of a variety of different types of contracts in an industry-friendly, while discerning and wise, manner.

Integrating behaviour change

Integrating the behaviour change efforts of governments, academia, industry and civil society is vital to enable lasting positive change. For example, decarbonising existing housing stock to improve energy efficiency is an important target for the UK government, who became the first government to create legally binding targets for a net zero-carbon future by 2050.

Already universities and local government are coming together, often around 'policy engagement'. The UCL Public Policy team and the UK's Local Government Association set up NZIP to bring together local authorities, universities, and other stakeholders to address climate change at the local level and seek routes to achieve council's net-zero commitments.[10] Deployment, implementation or 'translation' of research related to net-zero innovation will become increasingly important, rather than merely publishing academic papers.

A possible scenario related to integrated behaviour change across sectors could be as follows. Central government provide funding to incentivise local authorities to implement retrofitting of social housing stock with energy-efficient measures such as cavity wall insulation. Universities choose to invest in retrofitting their student accommodation to comply with legislation, or as a tactical measure to move up the 'impact rankings'. Other pilot projects are funded to promote innovation in community heating following a call for proposals from government. Universities with expertise in new energy storage and delivery technologies such as hydrogen boilers or biodigesters are then approached by a pioneering developer, construction company or charity about developing innovative solutions for a small area, to leverage government innovation funding. Once a demonstrator project has been set up – measuring reduction in CO_2, for example – wider awareness of the potential of such technologies among civil society takes place and greater investment from the private sector occurs.

Tool – How to negotiate a Minimum Viable Partnership

Everything on Earth is made of a mix of just 118 substances called 'elements', 92 of which are natural and 26 are made by humans. Humans themselves are made from 28 elements, of which carbon forms 20 per cent of an individual's body. Just as elements cannot be broken down into more simple ingredients, we think that the elemental concept of MVP is useful when thinking about forming alliances.

Many will be familiar with the term 'Minimum Viable Product'; however, it is vital that leaders within KE consider the MVP that you wish to develop with a company. This concept can help with planning, negotiation, implementation and performance management by ensuring you simplify your relationships to what is essential to create or add mutual value. There is no 'one size fits all' in terms of the outputs of this, as KE and partnership building is context-specific. However, we would expect the following institutional assets and attitudes to be present in an MVP from both the academic and industrial side.

Firstly, there must be an 'opportunity' or problem to be addressed that people really care about. There needs to be a desire, shared interest, and the ambition to mobilise and solve such problems. Is there compatibility and alignment? 5th generation universities will use the UN SDGs to help frame these problems in the glocal context.

Secondly, you need agreement on up to three objectives for the partnership (summarised in three sentences) and what the mutual and societal benefits of the collaboration should be. This is where there needs to be a good understanding of what resources or assets the university can offer. Within the UK, most universities are publicly funded and have charitable status and therefore must recognise their responsibilities for societal benefit through their activities.

Thirdly, a cost-benefit analysis and due diligence or risk assessment must be completed. Ideally this should happen proactively before approaching the partner, rather than reactively. For universities, this should include reading investor reports and company websites, and learning about the company's values and track record working with universities and other partners.

Fourthly, the prospective partner must have the organisational readiness and capability to arrange and sustain a productive relationship in the agreed timescale.

Finally, the alliance team in the company should have an open and flexible attitude with a credible and dedicated alliance lead. It can be useful for them to have sectoral knowledge. For universities we recommend there is both an academic lead as well as a strategic alliance manager who is well connected internally, who will record interactions in a CRM system. There needs to be regular, peer-to-peer communication including between Executive Champions.

Case study: a climate tech accelerator incorporating entrepreneurship training and innovation

In March 2016, a strategic alliance leader within an engineering faculty of a leading global university in the Global North realised, from desk-based research as well as discussions with academic and industry colleagues, that the leader's faculty could have a significant impact on digital innovation in agriculture and climate change more broadly.

The leader recognised that several UN SDGs were relevant for AgTech innovation such as zero hunger (SDG 2), climate change (SDG 13) and life on land (SDG 15). The faculty had significant expertise in areas such as the Internet of Things (IoT) and AI, but very little experience working with the agriculture sector. The leader saw a need and an opportunity to form a mutually beneficial strategic alliance to draw on complementary expertise and assets with a prominent agricultural research institute, located only a short distance from a major urban area. The institute had agile business incubation space and a track record of high-impact agricultural research.

How can technological innovation help feed the world's rapidly growing population? Farms of all sizes in the developed and developing world need better yields and fewer losses, and retailers require better-quality forecasts, resilience and integrity of supply. Following a period of strategic thinking and foresight planning, the leader reached out to a counterpart within the alliance function at the institute.

Following discussions, both leaders recognised the complementary assets of each of their respective organisations and the opportunity to collaborate in achieving significantly more through partnership than they could alone. They scoped out collaboration opportunities and alignment with university and institute priorities and overall strategic goals. They then did the following over the next year:

• They delivered a consultation event on Ag-Tech IoT and Precision Agriculture with 70 experts from industry and academia at the university's tech incubator space, to identify industry challenges and needs.

- They arranged reciprocal visits between the university and the institute to discuss opportunities to support the development of an Ag-Tech IoT research and innovation programme.
- They initiated five MSc student projects between the university and the institute.
- They applied successfully for internal seed funding from the University for KE and innovation activities.
- They jointly set up a PhD and Early Career Researcher entrepreneurship programme and hackathon. This focused on supporting farmers in the Global South with training and support from international development charities.
- They organised a training programme on lean entrepreneurship and social enterprise business models explaining how so many of the UN SDGs can be tackled through new agricultural technologies and solutions for farmers and other parts of the food supply chain. They attracted students from multiple disciplines to form teams and co-develop solutions for agriculture. The students took part in a 'Dragons' Den'-style competition. The competition helped to bring together academic and professional services staff from the two institutions and to grow mutual trust.
- Student start-ups created during the competition successfully applied for research funding for projects related to supporting rice farmers in the Philippines and cassava farmers in Nigeria.

The key lessons learned by the leaders from both organisations in this case were of the importance of gaining high-level executive support and buy-in through matched funding for staff time. This demonstrated that the university and the institute were both fully committed to the alliance. There was also a culture of small-scale experimentation with different KE pathways.

In a matter of two years, with senior-level management 'champions' from the University's Vice Dean (Enterprise) and Dean, and strong communication through open peer-to-peer relationships with the Institute's Director, the alliance expanded to include two other regional universities. It went on to secure £2.7m European Regional Development Funding (ERDF) and £3.5m from a corporate philanthropic foundation to set up a climate tech accelerator with a focus on AgTech circular economy solutions. The accelerator supports social entrepreneurs through business and technical mentoring and provides access to investors. The accelerator targets several UN SDGs including climate change (SDG 13). The university alliance team involved won an award from the university's president in recognition of their innovative entrepreneurial approach to this world-class alliance.

In summary, this case study shows how a partnership can start from small beginnings and, with the right people with a strong vision and shared values, can have a transformational strategic impact, contributing to the UN SDGs and achieving deeper collaboration between the Global North and Global South.

Lessons learned

- 5th generation universities have the resources, tools, systems, incentives and processes in place to scale their impact globally to contribute collaboratively created solutions to the biggest future challenges for our planet. They are purpose-driven organisations that can think 5th generationally, and have demonstrated how they contribute for the global public good.
- Executing sustainable relationships requires 'realising' consistent benefits and value from collaboration, and 'releasing' value to partners through the alliance. This is what we mean by 'mutual benefit'.
- KE and alliance leaders can use the concept of 'Minimum Viable Partnership' (MVP) to start to develop an effective relationship with a corporate. This concept can effectively help with planning, implementation, and performance management. Ensure you simplify relationships to what is essential to add value.
- Collaborative execution requires a unique and well-developed skillset and proactive attitude that understands how to work collaboratively through MVPs to deliver PoC demonstrators.
- People are the most critical factor to achieve the organisational change necessary for transitioning to a 5th generation university that can be a hotspot for transformational collaborative innovation.
- Leaders in 5th generation universities can develop, grow and maintain sustainable relationships and execute transformational

strategic alliances for global public good. They can operate across institutional and disciplinary boundaries, bringing together the right people with the right resources to create and deliver innovative solutions.

- Strategic alliance professionals must seek to build resilience into their value propositions, underpinning alliances so they can deal with inevitable change. This requires creating flexible structures that can cope with disruption.

- Driving positive and transformational change requires leaders to be strategic thinkers who are prepared to take risks and innovate around their organisation's operational management and business models. 5th generation universities will have a strong brand for being 'purpose-driven' institutions that are focused on their institutional mission, vision and values and are prepared to engage externally to advance these.

- 5th generation universities will consider how they can advance both global research and development together in alliance with industry, to achieve societal benefit. They do this through aligning their leaders and the different logics and discourse of university and industry participants through longer-term mutually beneficial relationships that advance shared goals, interests and priorities.

- The UN SDGs provide a helpful framework for developing aligning conversations that either support core interests or protect and de-risk against systemic negative changes such as the existential threats posed by climate change.

- The journey from strategy to execution involves consideration of resource management, how to build strong alliance functionality and multi-sector teams with technical, business and end-user representatives. The quintuple helix concept provides an effective paradigm for the most transformational university–industry alliances to emerge.

- Government can facilitate university–industry-civil society roundtable events to discuss the intersection of technology trends, societal impacts, innovation and regulatory roadmaps. This is a challenge- or mission-oriented ecosystem approach to achieving positive change at scale. Universities can bring to bear a multidisciplinary, evidence-based perspective for these discussions that can help to establish focus areas for collaboration and set boundaries and direction for transformational alliances to grow.

- Execution in a 5th generation university will mean moving from understanding the perceived benefits of an alliance to realisation of benefits both internally and externally. This is a non-linear process of building trust through effective communication and initiatives that de-risk the alliance for all stakeholders, both internally and externally. This will achieve a result that is greater than the sum of the parts. In other words, the alliance allows both organisations to achieve more together than they could by working alone.

- When academics lose a connection in their research and teaching to the long-term mission and strategy of the university, their relationships with industry are unlikely to be sustainable and beneficial for the university.

5

Looking into the future:
the next decade

What distinguishes leaders from others is that they
not only have an interest in the future, they also have
the capacity to deal with the future. This capacity is
sometimes called 'foresight'.

Tom Marshall, from his book
Understanding Leadership[1]

5th generation universities form alliances that look to the future
and seek to have an impact both nationally and globally to bring
about positive change. Leaders of 5th generation universities must
have foresight.

In the early 1870s, a group of Methodists were holding a
convention on the campus of Hartsville College, Indiana. The
College President started the conference by sharing his vision
for society: "We live in an exciting age, the age of inventions."
He explained to the ministers present how he thought that
people would one day fly from place to place instead of riding
horses. However, a man named Bishop Milton Wright stood
up in protest: "Heresy! The Bible says that flight is reserved for
the angels! We will have no such talk at this conference." He
continued to say that if God had intended man to fly, He would
have given him wings. The Bishop collected his two young sons,
Orville and Wilbur, and left.[2]

About 30 years later, on 17 December 1903, the Wright
brothers made the first powered flight, something their father
once thought was impossible to achieve. As university leaders in

a new era of existential threats facing humanity and our planet, will we be prepared to take risks to bring about positive change for the benefit of all our futures? Or will we prefer to remain in our comfort zones, in Museums of Procrastination, tied to old ways and traditions of how universities should work?

Intriguingly, Bishop Wright bought a cork toy for his boys when they were seven and eleven years old that resembled a helicopter, with a propeller driven by a rubber band. The toy had sparked the boys' imagination and a lifelong interest in flight. The boys became bicycle mechanics and, despite many failures in their experiments with gliders, on 17 December, Orville made history, flying 120 feet in 12 seconds, and then later in the day, Wilbur flew for 59 seconds. Their story teaches us that we should never underestimate what is possible. In 1910, Bishop Wright who had now become supportive of his boys' incredible aviation efforts, flew with Orville for seven minutes at an altitude of 350 feet.[3]

5th generation universities will be open minded and form alliances that look to the future. They will seek to have an impact locally, nationally, and globally as they seek to create more inclusive, sustainable, and resilient societies. They have rediscovered their identity as a public good and demonstrate real value for society at different scales. While they may face opposition, they are prepared to take calculated risks through innovative, new alliances with diverse industry sectors and beyond.

University leaders need foresight

Foresight is the ability or capacity to deal effectively with the future. How do university leaders become better at pointing their institution in the direction of future-proofing their organisations?

University leaders with foresight have vision for how universities can make a better world. They can creatively identify future opportunities and possibilities and proactively respond to these with agility. In this sense, they are entrepreneurial, intuitive and future-orientated. They can see how the global pandemic has significantly changed the landscape of higher education worldwide and how universities must adapt. They sense where opportunities are going to appear, and their intuitions have been proved right in many cases previously.

The future is hidden in the present, and next generation leaders with foresight are often able to 'see' this more clearly than others and act to realise possibilities. They anticipate future needs and respond to these. University leaders with foresight will be prepared to implement a strategy that is willing to make big changes, including abandoning old ways of doing things.

Some leading corporations with strong foresight implement a 'work backwards' approach to developing new products and services. This involves working backwards from the ideal end solution for customers. They start by writing a mock 'press release' about a finished product, enabling developers to visualise what this may look like and to decide whether the product is worth building. The process encourages a focus on alignment with desired impact and outcomes, ensuring that adequate project management and resourcing can be provided.

What if university leaders involved their customers or end users to visualise an ideal end state for their institutions? This would, of course, include their students and their industry funders, who would be invited to write 'press releases' about the future shape of their institutions. What shape of future university would emerge in the 'press release' for your academic institution? Would it highlight a university eager to have a transformational impact leading to positive change in the world?

In the rest of this chapter, we will highlight several key trends that we think will shape the coming decade for universities. We are expecting to see further rapid changes that will lead to the growth of 5th generation universities.

Changing approaches to strategic corporate philanthropy

Philanthropy through both corporates and foundations is likely to continue to grow funded research to address the big challenges facing humanity. Such 'impact investing' will become an increasingly important funding source for universities as public funding reduces and will require universities to become more entrepreneurial, aligning their university research and venturing with corporate venturing and philanthropic goals.

Universities will need to be more flexible in their discussions around IP, with a blurring between pure philanthropy and an increase in 'venture philanthropy' funding research from gifts that have some strings attached. These strings will be more condition-based in terms of whether certain deliverables have been met and stated impacts related to specified UN SDGs realised. Philanthropically 'viable' projects will only be undertaken if they align and contribute to the university's mission, vision and values. For 5th generation universities, this will mean they will have a strong focus on addressing the Global Goals, through multi-sector alliances that are transformational for all organisations involved.

The donor journey of a corporate for philanthropy has traditionally looked like Figure 5.1, driven by either the donor, the institution or the academic. We are already seeing that corporates are becoming less transactional and more ambitious with their philanthropy, partnering with universities that have aligned values and ambitions. 5th generation universities that

Figure 5.1: The traditional university approach to corporate philanthropy

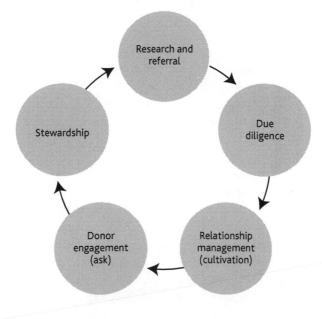

have set their sights on deeper, longer-term strategic and multifaceted alliances will be best placed to attract these resources.

A UK report on corporate philanthropy titled 'From transactional to transformative' states: 'Charities, universities and cultural organisations are likely to face important decisions about whether to embrace more complex and multifaceted collaborations, or to pursue more the modest (and increasingly rare) rewards of traditional philanthropic transactions.'[4]

For a 5th generation university, the donor journey will look more like Figure 5.2. This new approach will focus on a more integrated, holistic, transformational and co-ventured philanthropy, involving corporate engagement activity more broadly that is not traditionally philanthropic in nature.

Figure 5.2: The 5th generation co-venture approach to strategic corporate philanthropy

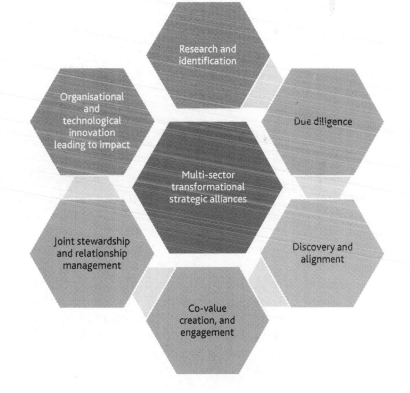

Trust, transparency and resilience and the growing importance of environmental, social and corporate governance criteria

During the pandemic, universities were forced to pivot very rapidly into a digital-based teaching and delivery model that was 'business critical'. Some were better prepared and more resilient than others and were able to rapidly scale their cloud computer resources and create a culture change among academic and professional staff to deliver a more online and blended learning experience.

Resilience to change and 'shocks' will become a topic of great concern among senior leaders of both universities and corporates over the next decade. There will be a greater focus on effective governance of external engagement activities to ensure they align with strong environmental, social and corporate governance (ESG) criteria.[5] These are intangible measures of the societal impact of organisations that are increasingly important for any organisation wishing to have a good credit rating internationally. Resilient universities will be those who adopt characteristics of a 5th generation university, such as a focus on digital transformation of university processes and systems through automation, creating a more agile and adaptable culture.

Greater focus on external engagement as a critical university function

Universities must never be seen as 'ivory towers', inaccessible and far removed from the reality of a suffering world. The post-pandemic era has created huge opportunities for external engagement with new industry partners, governments, NGOs, charities and philanthropic foundations worldwide, as well as between Global North and Global South universities. This will lead to a more inclusive and equitable global academia and will give prominence to a wider range of voices, including from groups representing indigenous people and those who are marginalised in society, for example, without access to education.

5th generation universities will become well known among governments, civil society, and industry for pioneering inclusive and responsible innovation, actively growing the number of start-ups with founders from under-represented backgrounds. There will be a greater desire for companies to leverage the talent of entrepreneurial students and academics rather than just secure IPR. This may lead to a shift away from TTOs being separate and physically removed from the main university campus, towards more integrated and embedded models of technology transfer that are located closer to academic staff and students.

Global South universities are often most exposed to the challenges to be addressed through the UN SDGs. These institutions offer immense value as collaborators for Global North universities and industry to achieve societal benefit for some of the world's poorest people. Greater transformational strategic alliances between the Global North and Global South higher education institutions and industry will require greater use of digital collaboration and translation tools. The VC of Uganda's leading Makerere University has said: 'I think there is a need now to approach collaboration on a more equal footing ... The universities in the developed countries might have more resources but intellectual capacity is not necessarily also only concentrated in the developed countries.'[6]

Non-traditional industry sectors will form university alliances

Alliances between universities and companies in sectors with historically low productivity and investment in R&D, such as carbon-intensive sectors including construction, logistics and agriculture, have the potential for mission-led sectoral transformation. This will include themes such as decarbonisation and increasing food security/resilience of supply chains. In addition, service industries, such as finance and insurance and experience-led industries such as gaming, sports, entertainment, tourism and leisure, are all ripe for new alliances with universities in their regions and beyond.

'Hyper-partnering' will become a phenomenon, with greater collective efforts than ever before across whole industries to partner with universities, even ones that are not in their own regions, who have complementary expertise, equipment and resources to tackle pervasive problems. The UK government wishes to stimulate a rise in the UK's research intensity with a goal of investing 2.4 per cent of GDP in R&D by 2027. To achieve this, they must facilitate and enable such hyper-partnering.[7]

Convergence research and innovation

5th generation universities will recognise the urgency to solve global goals and the need to accelerate discovery of solutions and delivery of societal benefits, both nationally and internationally. No single academic discipline or sector can tackle such challenges alone and so there will be a greater convergence or coming together of diverse, multidisciplinary, novel ideas and technologies. This will result in greater research valorisation, producing viable solutions and social innovation. New transformational models of multi-sector collaboration will emerge that will most likely be government-funded, with 5th generation universities as the key driving force. They will enable greater insights from a wider range of voices, recognising the role of researchers from both inside and outside academia, for example, those in corporate R&D labs.

University procurement will become more holistically focused

Universities will look for more from their major suppliers than just procurement in a purely transactional approach. Rather, they will leverage their supplier relationships as a means of creating, realising and releasing value – both mutual value and value for wider society. For example, they will encourage the transition to a more sustainable, zero-carbon economy through making use of the purchasing power and influence of their institutions.

Lifelong learning and micro-credentials will become more important

According to an analysis by McKinsey & Company for the Confederation of British Industry (CBI), nine out of every ten employees will need to reskill by 2030.[8] This will lead to significant change in the business models of many universities. They will become increasingly driven by students and employer needs for lifelong learning and upskilling. They must shed their image as 'graduate factories', instead creating learners who will return to university throughout their careers, through offering both short courses with certification as well as conventional degrees of at least 1–3 years normally.

5th generation universities will lead by example in providing good access to education for their own staff. They will have a culture of offering free or significantly discounted access to study and training opportunities for their own employees to demonstrate that they value and invest in their own talent, improving the resilience of the university to disruption by equipping their staff with important future skills. These will include collaboration, foresight, circular economy thinking, and adaptive leadership.

Curriculum co-design and workforce development

Talent from multidisciplinary teaching programmes bridging the STEM/non-STEM divide will become increasingly important in the post-pandemic era where companies are dependent upon a wider range of skills than is conventionally taught within one subject area. This is likely to lead to greater involvement of corporates, public health bodies and other civil society organisations in the co-design of the structure and content of repeatable, credit-based, certified teaching programmes aimed at professionals. This may include the creation of bespoke short courses, as well as longer programmes to upskill employees in new areas of technology such as AI. These courses are likely to also include a greater focus on responsible innovation, for example the ethical implications of the development of these technologies and the trend towards greater automation impacting whole industries.

Bespoke programmes for workforce development generally require a framework collaboration agreement to be in place between the university and the industry partner. The objectives of industry in collaborating with universities to run these programmes are to upskill employees as well as to attract and retain talent in an increasingly competitive knowledge economy.

A leading US technology corporation and its co-founder made a $50m combined gift to a US university in 2020 encompassing hardware, software, training and services. The gift focused on workforce development in the AI space as well as collaborative research. The gift will enable a multifaceted and integrated engagement through research, teaching, schools' outreach and workforce development to foster a deeper understanding of AI among their workforce. On top of this strategic corporate philanthropy, the university invested another $20m in new buildings for supercomputer facilities. This type of blended and co-venture philanthropy will increasingly become the norm in future.

The growing social innovation function of universities

The African Union and the European Union both have a strong interest in university–industry alliances related to the UN SDGS. The African Union's Agenda 2063 sets out priority areas linked to the SDGs,[9] and the Continental Education for Africa (CESA 16-25) policy document that forms part of this highlights as one of its pillars the importance of strong multi-sector partnerships.[10] CESA also has objectives to:

- 'build win-win partnerships between tertiary and vocational training institutions and enterprises to jointly develop and implement relevant curricula and programmes'; and
- 'revitalise and expand tertiary education, research and innovation to address continental challenges and promote global competitiveness'.

In his book *Impact: Reshaping Capitalism to Drive Real Change*,[11] philanthropist, venture capitalist and social innovator Sir Ronald Cohen, a pioneer of the impact investment movement, has highlighted how many investors are now more interested than ever in achieving social impact through their investments. This is about investment beyond mere monetary return alone. 5th generation universities will embed entrepreneurialism and social innovation into their curriculum and also provide support through accelerators to help students to set up their own companies during their degree.

In the West, innovation labs pursuing social innovation and entrepreneurship are a trend that will accelerate. Transformational strategic alliances will involve both researchers and students within universities and their start-up and spin-out ecosystems working together with industry to solve societal challenges.

5th generation universities will scale up their innovation-focused activities such as accelerators, and their alliances focused on commercialisation. However, TTOs will need to expand their focus to include more social enterprises as well as more traditional commercial business models. Bolder licensing agreements for public good will also become a feature of the landscape over the next decade impacting TTOs.

Capacity-building and greater cooperation across disciplines, cultures and countries

While geopolitical rivalry in recent years has become more intense, there is hope that critical global grand challenges such as climate change may provide a means to bring countries together to find solutions for positive change. Universities will boost their capacity for alliances at different scales. The role of KE and KE professionals will grow in profile among governments globally. There will become an increasing number of university staff who exist in non-binary, hybrid academic roles.

Some governments have started to notice the vital role of KE practitioners in universities, for example, the UK R&D Roadmap states: 'Productive interaction between the business and academic communities is often impeded by a shortage of relevant knowledge and skills in research translation and entrepreneurship.'[12]

Tomas Coates Ulrichsen's report for the National Centre for Universities and Business (NCUB)[13] assessing the effects of COVID-19 on how universities contribute to innovation, found that UK universities are placing much greater emphasis on:

- challenge-driven programmes and Centres of Excellence that integrate research and further development into applications (innovation);
- supporting companies to develop new innovations, and adopt the latest innovations to drive productivity;

- working to convene/better connect organisations to innovate (networks);
- building entrepreneurial and innovation capabilities and cultures (locally, sectors or technologies);
- providing leadership and intelligence to shape the strategic direction of places, sectors and technologies.

The report also highlighted that universities are placing greater importance on building multi-stakeholder ecosystems or consortia and collaborations to address critical challenges facing society and industries. To achieve this will involve building the skills and expertise of researchers as well as KE professionals so they can collaborate more effectively with industry. 5th generation universities will bring together cross- and transdisciplinary knowledge and expertise and integrate a range of different ideas and approaches to achieve positive change. Professional associations such as UIDP, UIIN and PraxisAuril can help to build capacity by training academics and students to engage more effectively with industry partners.

Grant funding for research and innovation projects involving alliances should factor in the staff time required to effectively manage and execute both the project and partnership. For instance, setting up cohort-based Centres for Doctoral Training (CDTs) is a model that has been very successful in the UK. These are co-funded by industry, government and academia.

Growth in international prizes and co-branded Centres of Excellence addressing societal challenges

These Centres of Excellence will be focused on broad areas of activity addressing societal challenges such as healthcare, inclusive education and climate change, rather than detailed, prescriptive challenges. Such prizes will incentivise academics globally and will become as prestigious as Nobel Prizes launched in the 19th century have become.

A global pharmaceutical company initiated the 'Future Insight Prize' in 2019 to give out up to one million euros annually for the next 35 years to:

stimulate innovative solutions to solve some of humanities greatest problems and to realise the dreams for a better tomorrow in the areas of health, nutrition and energy. The Future Insight Prize will put the vision for ambitious dream products of global importance for humankind into the world and will trigger curiosity and creativity worldwide on how to make this vision a reality[14]

Inspired by President John F. Kennedy's 'Moon Shot', the Duke and Duchess of Cambridge launched the international Earthshot Prize in October 2021 'designed to incentivise change and help repair our planet over the next ten years' through working together. It is centred around five 'Earthshots' that seek to 'improve life for us all, for generations to come' by taking solutions to scale through urgent innovation from multinational teams. It will award five, £1m prizes each year for the next ten years, providing at least 50 solutions to the world's greatest environmental problems by 2030.[15] The five challenges to be overcome are:

1. Protect and restore nature
2. Clean our air
3. Revive our oceans
4. Build a waste-free world
5. Fix our climate

The international media attention and prestige of such awards will help to galvanise a new interest and momentum among academics to collaborate across sectors and develop innovative solutions to global challenges.

Greater government and public recognition of universities in economic recovery

The role of universities in economic and social recovery will be increasingly recognised by the public, as 5th generation universities emerge that will have rediscovered the contribution they can make as a public good to social innovation and positive change. This will be driven partly by the publicity that they gain from the central role they will play in leading and executing transformational strategic alliances with industry, as well as with other multi-sector partners.

The public are increasingly recognising the crucial role that universities have in economic growth and recovery post-pandemic, and this is reflected by policy-makers in, for example, the UK and US governments' Build Back Better strategies as well as within various African Union and European Union strategies.

It is likely that the contribution that universities make to wider innovation ecosystems through training future entrepreneurs will also be more widely recognised. What is less clear is whether the vital but often hidden highly skilled role of KE practitioners and alliance leaders in releasing value to wider society and driving positive change will be better understood and appreciated. It is hoped that this book will be a step in making that vision a reality.

Tool – Foresight planning for United Nations Sustainable Development Goal 17, partnerships for the goals

If you wish to see the future of your university emerging from the present, you will need to encourage your university staff from across different disciplines and professional service functions to see the potential for transformational strategic alliances to bring positive change in the world. The DISRUPT tool shown below in Figure 5.3 can help to encourage disruptive innovative thinking about how to achieve UN SDG 17, partnership for the goals, and make positive change a reality in your institution.

This tool should be used within a multidisciplinary and ideally multi-sector 'sandbox' workshop session to run during

Figure 5.3: Levers of influence for transformation between different sectors

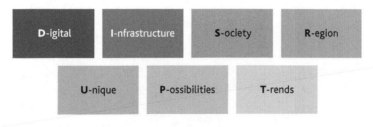

a morning or afternoon (half-day). During such a session, we recommend there is an introduction by a member of the university leadership team to highlight the importance of the UN SDGs for the institution.

We recommend the workshop has no more than about 35 people and that there are seven tables with up to five people per table representing different academic disciplines, professional services teams and guests from industry, government, and civil society. Each table should have a large letter representing each of the categories within the word D.I.S.R.U.P.T (defined below), for example Table 'D', Table 'I' and so on. It is also useful for each table to have a card with graphics summarising all 17 UN SDGs. Each table will have a whiteboard. The group should discuss, explore and record their ideas about how the university can work together across disciplines and sectors to achieve its university mission and vision through an integrated and holistic approach to research, teaching and innovation.

Every ten minutes, the people at each table will rotate to another table so they cover all seven tables throughout the session. The tool facilitates conversations and uncovers interesting insights and perspectives from diverse cross-sector stakeholders.

There should also be training provided for academic and professional services staff and guests covering topics such as: team science (meaning STEM and non-STEM together); human centred design; systems thinking; the circular economy; storytelling; pitching; and inclusive, responsible and 'frugal' innovation.

Here is an explanation of each of the boxes shown in Figure 5.3:

- *Digital* – consider how digital technologies are transforming the university internally and how they can bring transformation externally to wider society, through alliances that achieve the UN SDGs.
- *Infrastructure* – consider how your university infrastructure (campus facilities) and built environment can provide opportunities for new alliances to address the UN SDGs.
- *Society* – consider how your university is seen in your society and how it can form alliances to achieve gender equality and inclusive positive change for all.

- *Region* – consider how your university is currently contributing to achieving the UN SDGs in your region and how it can achieve more through alliances.
- *Unique* – consider what is unique about the university and how all the university's assets can complement those from different backgrounds and sectors.
- *Possibilities* – set your mind free to explore all the possibilities of new alliances to achieve the UN SDGs, between different academic disciplines that have not worked much together before as well as from across different sectors.
- *Trends* – consider the current political, economic, sociological, technological, legal, and environmental trends that may enable new ways of working together to achieve the UN SDGs.

Case study – Horizon Europe and Transition Super-Labs: accelerating the transition to a zero-carbon economy in the EU through multi-sector alliances

In 2018, a High-Level Panel (HLP) Report of the European Decarbonisation Initiative was produced for the European Commission, following two years of work by a team of nine experts. The report described the necessary actions to achieve decarbonisation across multiple industries and a transition to a zero-carbon economy by 2050.

There were several interesting recommendations in the report, which described an integrated approach covering several crosscutting themes relevant to the EU Framework Programme for Research and Innovation 2021–27, known as 'Horizon Europe':

- the need for continuous research and innovation (R&I) activities on decarbonisation across all sectors, including a strong focus on climate change science;
- the establishment of large crosscutting, transdisciplinary, and mission-oriented programmes that integrate systemic innovation alongside research;
- the development of industry alliances to address together the most difficult aspects of decarbonisation, on which industry alone would not invest enough or act with the necessary urgency;

- the launch of 'Transition Super-Labs', an interesting 'living lab' concept about large-scale initiatives of real-life management of the transition from fossil-fuel-based local economies to zero-carbon ones.

The Transition Super-Lab concept (Figure 5.4) resonates with our thinking about the need for demonstrators that engage with multi-sector organisations through transformational strategic alliances. These sector-leading, flagship demonstrators combine the best of academia, industry, government and civil society to co-produce integrated solutions that deliver real value and societal benefit.

The urgency and complexity of SDG 13, climate change, requires the need for a large-scale testbed environment that will enable stakeholders to experiment together, using all the

Figure 5.4: Conceptual representation of Transition Super-Labs: large territorial initiatives for fostering the transition to a zero-carbon economy in particularly vulnerable areas

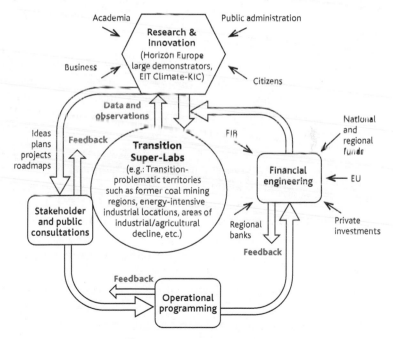

Source: European Commission[16]

195

levels of influence (Figure 4.1) to make a transformational impact on accelerating the zero-carbon transition. These testbeds should be in areas where local and regional economies are heavily dependent on fossil fuels to gain widespread buy-in to technologies that will create the 'green jobs' of the future. There should be a strong focus from universities in these regions, where there may be significant mining activity or carbon-intensive industry for example, on upskilling and entrepreneurship through accelerators that will also attract the impact investment community.

Evidence suggests that decarbonisation at pace and scale happens only through systemic solutions within advanced industrialised societies. In other words, a transformational approach to disrupting whole industry sectors is required and alliances have a vital role to play here, alongside highly visible 'living lab' environments where theory can be tested in a practical way and innovation can be implemented, monitored and revised in line with insights gained via a systems engineering, team science and human-focused, design-centric approach.

Lessons learned

- Almost every industry is facing disruption and transformation through an Industry 4.0 convergence of technologies such as AI, quantum computing and synthetic biology. This creates great opportunities for innovation and collaboration between universities and industry to bring about positive change as well as the advancement of science.
- Government and regulatory changes to encourage greener economic growth also present great potential for universities to leverage in the transition to a zero-carbon world. Governments can create enabling environments for long-term, multi-sector, mission-driven collaboration to be fostered and scaled for societal benefit, putting into practice ideas and solutions to achieve positive social change.
- Universities must not be on the wrong side of history or seen as out-of-date and out-of-touch with real world, existential social, environmental, and economic challenges.

- 5th generation universities will:
  - value innovation and the 'third mission' of universities as much as research and teaching. They see how engagement with partners in and through research and teaching is essential;
  - prioritise multidisciplinary research and teaching, and look to leverage the social sciences and humanities as well as engineering disciplines to tackle pressing societal challenges;
  - gain recognition from policy-makers in government for their ability to deliver the innovation infrastructure that supports regional economies to release and realise value;
  - gain growing public recognition for their multi-sector engagement to deliver societal benefits such as addressing the UN SDGs.
- Corporations across whole industries will increasingly see the value of strategic alliances with leading universities and form pre-competitive consortia to tackle specific challenges and set standards and regulations in the transition to a zero-carbon economy. Governments have an important role to facilitate this
- University licensing and TTOs will increasingly prioritise impact on humanity over commercialisation metrics alone, and will make it easier for industry to license technology. For example, this may be through new digital tools, such as online licensing platforms, to address challenges such as the climate emergency (SDG 13) and to provide more equitable access to technology. They will need to adjust their business models that are too focused on STEM disciplines to better support a growing range of entrepreneurial academics from the social sciences, the humanities and creative industries.
- 5th generation universities will increasingly look to take equity in promising student start-ups and spinouts with value in-kind through staff time commitment and expertise. They will also be great enablers of entrepreneurship among PhD students and postdocs, particularly through creating cohorts of entrepreneurs with access to training and mentoring from established 'Entrepreneurs in Residence'. They will provide flexible office space in university accelerators or science parks. There will be a significant growth of interest from universities in attracting a new wave of impact investors.

- Great ideas and innovation are found in both Global North and Global South universities, with brilliant talent everywhere. Greater alliances between Global North and Global South around innovation and entrepreneurship will create significant economic growth at different scales. A greater number of ambitious international collaborations between global academia and industry will lead to better research and teaching and more inclusive access to higher education worldwide.

- Universities will rediscover their nature as a 'public good' for the 'common good' of humanity within their mission and will start to gain a greater vision of creating positive change in the world through a holistic approach to research partnerships, teaching, student and staff entrepreneurship, philanthropy, consultancy and technology commercialisation. Their focus will not be self-interest and revenue maximisation, rather longer-term thinking focused on creating a better world for future generations.

- Universities will increasingly value diverse approaches to innovation: diversity across disciplinary areas (STEM/non-STEM), as well as diversity in innovation (incremental/frugal/disruptive). 5th generation universities adopt an integrated, multifaceted and multidimensional (heterogenous) approach to innovation.

Conclusion

5th generation universities will be very diverse in their size, socioeconomic context, geography, and sphere of influence. Some will be internationally well-known Russell Group (UK) or Ivy League (US) research-intensive universities. Others will be academic institutions in other parts of the world, both in the Global North and in the Global South, that may be very focused on excellence in teaching rather than predominantly research. What unites such universities, however, will be an integration of their core activities with operations focused on transformation, innovation and positive change. To achieve this, they will be highly collaborative, forming robust partnerships across sectors, including with industry, to achieve the 17 UN SDGs and create a better world for everyone, such as addressing the existential threat posed by climate change.

In this book we have developed the theory and practice of a new type of digitally enabled and agile university that is starting to emerge on the world stage. Currently we are only seeing aspects of the 5th generation university among a small but diverse group of institutions. It is our hope that academic institutions in the future will become even more inclusive, relevant and effective at tackling the biggest challenges facing humanity. They will utilise all the levers of influence within their quintuple helix of alliances, including with industry, government and civil society, bringing about positive change to their environment.

Academic leaders with foresight should recognise the importance of enduring, trusted and impactful university–industry partnerships that enable them to achieve far more together than they could ever do on their own. They will empower their staff, including both academic and non-academic KE practitioners, to be industry-aware and to demonstrate how the university's work makes a positive contribution to society. As part of achieving the academic mission, they will explore how to develop 'Professors of Practice' who can help to integrate industry insights and entrepreneurial understanding into their teaching programmes.

University–industry partnerships will form in an increasingly accelerated period, thanks to the advancement of digital collaboration technologies effectively used by all parties globally. 5th generation universities will also have a deeper understanding of the skills needed to develop, implement and lead alliances that move quickly beyond the transactional towards the transformational. These alliances will deliver sustainable value, impact across the UN SDGs both locally and globally (glocally), responsible research and innovation combined with societal benefit. This will be achieved through transdisciplinary programmatic activities and corporate philanthropy that delivers tangible and significant shared value. There has never been a better time for universities and industry to bring positive change for the world.

Bibliography

Baaken, T. and Schröder, C. (2008) 'The Triangle for Innovation in Technology Transfer at University of Applied Sciences', in K. Laine, P. van der Sijde, M. Lähdeniemi and J. Tarkkanen (eds) *Higher Education Institutions and Innovation in the Knowledge Society*, Helsinki, pp 103–16.

Baaken, T., Davey, T., Francis, A. and Kliewe, T. (2008) 'A Model for the Assessment and Extraction of Entrepreneurial Value from University Research', in Sarah Ingle and Marja-Liisa Neuvonen-Rauhala (eds) *Promoting Entrepreneurship by Universities*, Proceedings of the 2nd International FINPIN Conference, Hämeenlinna, Finland, 20–22 April 2008, pp 204–12.

Chan Kim, W. and Mauborgne, Renée (2017) *Blue Ocean Shift: Beyond Competing – Proven Steps to Inspire Confidence and Seize New Growth*, New York: Hachette Books.

Dottore, A., Baaken, T. and Corkindale, D. (2010) 'A Partnering Business Model for Technology Transfer: The Case of the Muenster University of Applied Sciences', *International Journal of Entrepreneurship and Innovation Management*, 12(2): 190–216. ISSN 1465-7503

Funcke, W., Groose, G., von Lojewski, U., Schröder, C. and Leonhardt, M.L. (2005) 'Transfer of Research and Knowledge at Münster University of Applied Sciences', Proceedings of 5th International Conference/Workshop on Science to Business Marketing and Successful Research Commercialisation, Tokyo, Japan, pp 395–406. www.science-marketing.com

Global Research and Development Expenditures: Fact Sheet, Congressional Research Service (updated 27 September 2021). https://fas.org/sgp/crs/misc/R44283.pdf

Notes

Preface

1. The Quintuple Helix innovation model: global warming as a challenge and driver for innovation (2012). Carayannis, E.G., Barth, T.D. and Campbell, D.F. *J Innov Entrep* 1, 2. https://doi.org/10.1186/2192-5372-1-2

2. For more information see 'University-Industry Collaboration: are SMEs different?' (2020). Andrew Johnston. *SOTA Review No 41* (June 2020).

Chapter 1

1. HSBC Procrastination Museum Advert by JWT (2015). https://www.youtube.com/watch?v=PVnUTp8t6EM

2. 'Academic R&D continues slow rise' (1 April 2020). Paul Heney, *R&D World*. https://www.rdworldonline.com/academic-rd-continues-slow-rise/

3. Study by Association of University Technology Managers (AUTM) (June 2017). Biotechnology Innovation Organisation. https://archive.bio.org/articles/value-academic-industry-partnerships

4. *Remix Strategy: The Three Laws of Business Combinations* (2015). Benjamin Gomes-Casseres. Harvard Business Review Press.

5. 'The Sustainable Development Agenda', United Nations. https://www.un.org/sustainabledevelopment/development-agenda-retired/

6. 'How to design a successful industrial strategy' (17 December 2020). Giles Wilkes. The Institute for Government. https://www.instituteforgovernment.org.uk/publications/industrial-strategy

7. European Market for Climate Services. European Commission. https://cordis.europa.eu/project/id/730500

8. *Open Innovation 2.0: A New Paradigm* (2013). Martin Curley and Bror Salmelin. https://ec.europa.eu/futurium/en/system/files/ged/24-oispgopeninnovation20anewparadigm-whitepaper.pdf

9. https://www.un.org/sustainabledevelopment/. The content of this publication has not been approved by the United Nations and does not reflect the views of the United Nations or its officials or Member States.

10. 'Devotions upon emergent occasions' (1624). Mediation XVII. John Donne.

11. https://www.un.org/sustainabledevelopment/. The content of this publication has not been approved by the United Nations and does not reflect the views of the United Nations or its officials or Member States.

12. 'What is knowledge exchange (KE)?' KE Concordat. https://support.keconcordat.ac.uk/about-the-ke-concordat/what-is-knowledge-exchange-ke

[13] 'The changing state of knowledge exchange: UK academic interactions with external organisations 2005–2015' (2016). Alan Hughes, Cornelia Lawson, Michael Kitson and Ammon Salter with Anna Bullock and Robert B. Hughes. NCUBx. https://www.ncub.co.uk/wp-content/uploads/2016/02/NCUB_The_Changing_State_of_Knowledge_Exchange_Feb16_WEB.pdf

[14] *Blue Ocean Strategy*. 2005.

[15] 'Moving to Blue Ocean Strategy: a five step process to make the shift' (24 September 2017). Steve Denning. https://www.forbes.com/sites/stevedenning/2017/09/24/moving-to-blue-ocean-strategy-a-five-step-process-to-make-the-shift/?sh=4f2288417f11

[16] Strategic Partnerships Office. University of Cambridge. https://www.strategic-partnerships.admin.cam.ac.uk/home/what-we-do

[17] *Better Business Better World* (January 2017). Business and Sustainable Development Commission. United Nations. https://sustainabledevelopment.un.org/index.php?page=view&type=400&nr=2399&menu=1515

[18] *Unlocking Digital Value to Society: A new framework for growth* (January 2017). WEF/Accenture. http://reports.weforum.org/digital-transformation/wp-content/blogs.dir/94/mp/files/pages/files/dti-unlocking-digital-value-to-society-white-paper.pdf

[19] Global Steering Group for Impact Investment. https://gsgii.org/2021/07/uk-creates-impact-taskforce-under-its-g7-presidency/

[20] Global Steering Group for Impact Investment. https://gsgii.org/2021/07/uk-creates-impact-taskforce-under-its-g7-presidency/

[21] Global Steering Group for Impact Investment. https://gsgii.org/2021/07/uk-creates-impact-taskforce-under-its-g7-presidency/

[22] Global Steering Group for Impact Investment. https://gsgii.org/2021/07/uk-creates-impact-taskforce-under-its-g7-presidency/

[23] Oxford Foundry. https://www.oxfordfoundry.ox.ac.uk/

[24] 'Effective policymaking to build the impact economy'. FutureLearn. https://www.futurelearn.com/courses/effective-policymaking-to-build-impact-economy

[25] 'UCL students win the Hult Prize 2018 claiming $1 million in seed funding for their social enterprise' (19 September 2018). https://www.ucl.ac.uk/enterprise/case-studies/2021/nov/ucl-alumni-tackle-food-poverty-worlds-first-sustainable-rice-brand

[26] Hult Prize. https://www.hultprize.org/

[27] 'Covid-19 is a chance to rebuild the reputation of universities' (3 November 2020). Rupert Younger. *Times Higher Education*. https://www.timeshighereducation.com/opinion/covid-19-chance-rebuild-reputation-universities

[28] *Strengthening the Contribution of English Higher Education Institutions to the Innovation System: Knowledge Exchange and HEIF Funding: A report for HEFCE* (2012). PACEC.

[29] *Towards the Third Generation University: Managing the University in Transition* (2009). J.G. Wissema. Edward Elgar.

30 Royal Academy of Engineering Africa Prize. https://www.raeng.org.uk/global/sustainable-development/africa-prize

31 'UP Vice Chancellor Prof Tawana Kupe awarded honorary doctorate by University of Montpellier'. Posted 7 October 2021. https://www.up.ac.za/news/post_3023997-up-vice-chancellor-prof-tawana-kupe-awarded-honorary-doctorate-by-university-of-montpellier

32 Times Higher Education Impact Rankings. https://www.timeshighereducation.com/impactrankings.

33 'Redeeming the Value of Higher Education' (6 March 2020). Centre for the Advancement of Christian Education (CACE). https://cace.org/redeeming-the-value-of-higher-education/

34 'Strategy and society: the link between competitive advantage and corporate social responsibility' (December 2006). *Harvard Business Review*. https://hbr.org/2006/12/strategy-and-society-the-link-between-competitive-advantage-and-corporate-social-responsibility

35 *Missions: A Beginner's Guide* (December 2019). M. Mazzucato and G. Dibb, UCL Institute for Innovation and Public Purpose. https://www.ucl.ac.uk/bartlett/public-purpose/publications/2019/dec/missions-beginners-guide

36 'Mission-oriented innovation'. UCL Institute for Innovation and Public Purpose website https://www.ucl.ac.uk/bartlett/public-purpose/research/mission-oriented-innovation

37 *Innovation in Translation: How Big Ideas Really Happen* (2021). Dave Ferrera. Forbes Books.

38 *Towards the third generation university: Managing the university in transition* (2009). J.G. Wissema. Edward Elgar.

39 'Successful universities towards the improvement of regional competitiveness: "fourth generation" universities'. 2013. Miklós Lukovics and Bence Zuti. https://econpapers.repec.org/RePEc:zbw:esconf:156762   EconStor Conference Papers, ZBW – Leibniz Information Centre for Economics.

40 'Knowledge exchange performance and the impact of HEIF in the English higher education sector'. Technical Report 2014. Tomas Coates Ulrichsen. DOI: 10.13140/RG.2.1.1748.4409.

41 *Where Good Ideas Come From* (2011). Steven Johnson. Penguin Publishing Group.

42 '68% average decline in species population sizes since 1970, says new WWF report' (9 September 2020). World Wildlife Fund. https://www.worldwildlife.org/press-releases/68-average-decline-in-species-population-sizes-since-1970-says-new-wwf-report

43 Carbon Disclosure Project (CDP) Report 2017. https://b8f65cb373b1b7b15feb-c70d8ead6ced550b4d987d7c03fcdd1d.ssl.cf3.rackcdn.com/cms/reports/documents/000/002/327/original/Carbon-Majors-Report-2017.pdf?1499691240

44 'Just 100 companies responsible for 71% of global emissions, study says' (10 July 2017). Tess Riley. *The Guardian*. https://www.theguardian.com/sustainable-business/2017/jul/10/100-fossil-fuel-companies-investors-responsible-71-global-emissions-cdp-study-climate-change

45 'Just 100 companies responsible for 71% of global emissions, study says' (10 July 2017). Tess Riley. *The Guardian*. https://www.theguardian.com/sustainable-business/2017/jul/10/100-fossil-fuel-companies-investors-responsible-71-global-emissions-cdp-study-climate-change

46 RE 100 Members, https://www.there100.org/re100-members

47 'Are universities and students aligned on sustainability priorities?'. July 5, 2021. Ellie Bothwell. *Times Higher Education*. https://www.timeshighereducation.com/world-university-rankings/are-universities-and-students-aligned-sustainability-priorities

48 'David W.C. MacMillan – Facts'. The Nobel Prize in Chemistry 2021. https://www.nobelprize.org/prizes/chemistry/2021/macmillan/facts/

49 'Princeton's David MacMillan receives Nobel Prize in chemistry'. (October 6, 2021). The Office of Communications. https://www.princeton.edu/news/2021/10/06/princetons-david-macmillan-receives-nobel-prize-chemistry

50 'From transactional to transformative: the future of corporate partnerships' (2018). Nik Miller. More Partnership. https://www.morepartnership.com/library/The_Future_of_Corporate_Partnerships.pdf

Chapter 2

1 *The Research University in Today's Society* (2017). Gerald Chan. UCL Press. Accessible at: https://www.uclpress.co.uk/products/94604

2 *The Civic University: The Policy and Leadership Challenges* (2016). Edited by John Goddard, Ellen Hazelkorn, Louise Kempton, and Paul Vallance. Edward Elgar.

3 'Creating the Innovative University' (2020). Randolph W. Hall. Technology and Innovation. Vol 21. pp 1–14. http://dx.doi.org/10,21300/21.4.2020.3

4 https://www.purdue.edu/research/industry-partners/resources/office-of-industry-partnerships-and-purdue.php

5 'The Competitive Advantage of Corporate Philanthropy' (2002). Michael E. Porter and Mark R. Kramer. *Harvard Business Review*. https://hbr.org/2002/12/the-competitive-advantage of-corporate-philanthropy

6 B Corporations are discussed later in Chapter 2.

7 'Dairy Milk, Ben & Jerry's and an Octopus' (14 April 2021). Octopus Group. https://octopusgroup.com/simon-rogerson-blog/octopus-b-corp/

8 Many universities signed up during the pandemic to put into practice the objectives of initiatives such as AUTM's COVID-19 Licensing Guidelines (https://autm.net/about-tech-transfer/covid19/covid-19-licensing-guidelines) and the COVID-19 Technology Access Framework (https://otl.stanford.edu/covid-19-technology-access-framework).

9 'About UCL-Ventura'. UCL Institute of Healthcare Engineering. https://www.ucl.ac.uk/healthcare-engineering/covid-19/ucl-ventura-breathing-aids-covid19-patients/about-ucl-ventura.

10 'Green jobs: the new generation of workers making it work for them'. David Shukman. https://www.bbc.co.uk/news/science-environment-58549135. BBC News Online accessed 15/9/21

11 NSF website: https://www.nsf.gov/
12 NSF https://www.nsf.gov/news/grc/grc_summary.jsp
13 'Responsible innovation'. UKRI. https://www.ukri.org/about-us/policies-standards-and-data/good-research-resource-hub/responsible-innovation/
14 *Mission Economy: A Moonshot Guide to Changing Capitalism* (2021). Mariana Mazzucato. Penguin Audio.
15 *Innovation in Real Places: Strategies for Prosperity in an Unforgiving World* (2021). Dan Breznitz. OUP USA.
16 'Want to be an innovation hot spot? Don't copy Silicon Valley' (9 February 2021). John Morgan. *Times Higher Education*. https://www.timeshigher education.com/news/want-be-innovation-hot-spot-dont-copy-siliconvalley
17 *Innovation in Real Places: Strategies for Prosperity in an Unforgiving World* (2021). Dan Breznitz. OUP USA
18 Cardiff University Social Science Research Park. https://www.cardiff.ac.uk/social-science-research-park
19 'Strategic Framework 2022'. Canterbury Christ Church University. https://www.canterbury.ac.uk/about-us/our-story/strategic-framework-2022
20 'Principles for Responsible Management Education'. United Nations https://www.unprme.org/what-we-do
21 'About B-Corps'. B Corporation. https://bcorporation.net/about-b-corps
22 B Corporation. https://bcorporation.net/
23 The Wellbeing Economy Alliance. https://weall.org/
24 'Why governments should prioritize well-being'. 2019. Nicola Sturgeon. https://www.ted.com/talks/nicola_sturgeon_why_governments_should_prioritize_well_being/transcript?language=en
25 'SDG Action Manager'. B Corporation. https://bcorporation.net/welcome-sdg-action-manager
26 *The Fifth Discipline: The Art and Practice of the Learning Organisation* (2006). Peter Senge. Random House Audio.
27 'Innovation ecosystems: greater than the sum of their parts?' (2019). Graca Carvalho, Alisdair Ritchie and Evan D. Fradkin. Published in: *Living in the Internet of Things* (Proceedings of IoT Conference, London, UK, 1–2 May 2019). ISBN 9781839530890. doi: http://dx.doi.org/10.1049/cp.2019.0151
28 'Redeeming the value of Higher Education' (6 March 2020). Centre for the Advancement of Christian Education (CACE) https://cace.org/redeeming-the-value-of-higher-education/
29 'A compassionate university'. University of Worcester. https://www.worcester.ac.uk/about/university-information/who-we-are/a-compassionate-university.aspx
30 *Towards the Compassionate University: From Golden Thread to Global Impact.* (2021). Edited by Kathryn Waddington. Routledge.
31 'The way forward for the UK's early stage innovation' (7 August 2021). Alice Gast, FT. https://www.ft.com/content/c73455ee-701a-4e60-8332-b3a316c45118

32 'Knowledge brokers need career paths too' (30 April 2021). Sarah Chaytor. UCL https://www.ucl.ac.uk/news/2021/apr/opinion-knowledge-brokers-need-career-paths-too

33 'Only 1% of UK university professors are black'. 19 January 2021. Sean Coughlan. BBC News https://www.bbc.co.uk/news/education-55723120

34 'Female leadership in top universities advances for first time since 2017' (6 March 2020). Ellie Bothwell. *Times Higher Education*. https://www.timeshighereducation.com/news/female-leadership-top-universities-advances-first-time-2017

35 Brilliant Minds Conference in Stockholm, 2019.

36 IPCC 2018 Special Report on the impacts of global warming of 1.5 degrees. https://www.ipcc.ch/sr15/

37 'Climate change widespread, rapid, and intensifying – IPCC' (9 August 2021). IPCC. https://www.ipcc.ch/2021/08/09/ar6-wg1-20210809-pr/

38 'E-scooter trial to be expanded to Salford Royal with 100,000 miles ridden so far' (28 July 2021). Joseph Timan. *Greater Manchester News*. https://www.manchestereveningnews.co.uk/news/greater-manchester-news/lime-e-scooter-trial-salford-21164452

39 Environmental Association for Universities and Colleges (EAUC). https://www.eauc.org.uk/. See Sustainability Scorecard at: https://www.eauc.org.uk/sustainability_leadership_scorecard

40 NSF's 10 Big Ideas. https://www.nsf.gov/news/special_reports/big_ideas/

41 NAE Grand Challenges for Engineering. http://www.engineeringchallenges.org/challenges.aspx

42 https://uidp.org/

43 'Special Message to the Congress on Urgent National Needs'. President John F. Kennedy. Delivered in person before a joint session of Congress on 25 May 1961. https://www.nasa.gov/vision/space/features/jfk_speech_text.html

44 Ellen MacArthur Foundation. https://ellenmacarthurfoundation.org/

45 'E = mc² equation'. Encyclopaedia Britannica. https://www.britannica.com/science/E-mc2-equation

46 UKRI Connecting Capability Fund – Research England. https://re.ukri.org/knowledge-exchange/the-connecting-capability-fund-ccf/

47 The Catapult Network in the UK. https://catapult.org.uk/

48 CaSE Report 'The Power of Place'. 12 May 2020. https://www.sciencecampaign.org.uk/resource/placereport.html#:~:text=Designed%20to%20feed%20into%20the,and%20nations%20of%20the%20UK

49 UK Government Department for Levelling Up, Housing and Communities https://www.gov.uk/government/organisations/department-for-levelling-up-housing-and-communities

50 'Universities as anchor institutions in cities in a turbulent funding environment: vulnerable institutions and vulnerable places in England' (2014). John Goddard, Mike Coombes, Louise Kempton and Paul Vallance. *Cambridge Journal of Regions, Economy and Society*, Vol 7, Issue 2, pp 307–25. https://doi.org/10.1093/cjres/rsu004

51 'Can a company live forever?' (19 January 2012). K. Gittleson. www.bbc. com/news/business-16611040

52 'The top 10 trends in tech – executive summary download' (June 2021). McKinsey & Company.https://www.mckinsey.com/~/media/McKinsey/ Business%20Functions/McKinsey%20Digital/Our%20Insights/The%20 top%20trends%20in%20tech%20final/Tech-Trends-Exec-Summary?mc_ cid=3d98b2fd1d&mc_eid=565ab91b44

53 State of the Markets EMEA report H1 2021. Silicon Valley Bank. https:// www.svb.com/uk/trends-insights/reports/state-of-the-markets-emea- report-h1-2021?mc_cid=3d98b2fd1d&mc_eid=565ab91b44

54 'The Unicorn Club'. Dealroom.co. https://app.dealroom.co/unicorns/f/ slug_locations/anyof_europe/tags/allof_verified%20unicorns%20 and%20%241b%20exits/year_became_unicorn_min/anyof_2021?mc_ cid=3d98b2fd1d&mc_eid=565ab91b44

55 'Winning formula: How Europe's top tech start-ups get it right' (18 August 2021). McKinsey & Company. https://www.mckinsey.com/industries/ technology-media-and-telecommunications/our-insights/winning- formula-how-europes-top-tech-start-ups-get-it-right?cid=soc-web&mc_ cid=3d98b2fd1d&mc_eid=565ab91b44

56 IDEALondon https://www.idealondon.co.uk/. Conception X: https:// conceptionx.org/. Oxford Foundry: https://www.oxfordfoundry.ox.ac. uk/. Cambridge Cluster: https://www.eastofengland.admin.cam.ac.uk/ cambridge-cluster

57 KE Concordat. https://www.keconcordat.ac.uk/

Chapter 3

1 Nelson Mandela often used this quote, but it is originally attributed to author Joel Arthur Barker, American Futurist from *The Power of Vision* (1991 video).

2 Pitchbook: https://pitchbook.com/

3 Crunchbase: https://www.crunchbase.com/

4 LinkedIn Sales Navigator: https://bit.ly/3pdybpt

5 Grant Forward: https://www.grantforward.com/search

6 Google Alerts https://www.google.co.uk/alerts

7 'Developmental sequence in small groups' (1965). Bruce Tuckman, *Psychological Bulletin*. Vol 63, no 6. pp 384–99. doi:10.1037/h0022100. PMID 14314073.

8 'Maximizing team performance: the critical role of the nurse leader' (1 January 2017). Kirstin Manges, Jill Scott-Cawiezell and Marcia M. Ward. *Nursing Forum*. Vol 52. No 1. pp 21–9. doi:10.1111/nuf.12161. ISSN 1744- 6198. PMID 27194144.

9 'Olympics cycling: Marginal gains underpin Team GB dominance' (8 August 2012). Matt Slater. BBC Sport.

10 'Nemawashi' in Wikipedia. https://en.wikipedia.org/wiki/Nemawashi

Chapter 4

1 *Develop Your Leadership Skills* (2007). John Adair. Kogan Page.
2 'Universities-industry collaboration, a systematic review' (2015). S. Ankrah and Q. Al-Tabbaa, *Scandi Journal of Management*, Vol 31 pp 387–408.
3 'Creativity is not enough' (1963). Theodore Levitt. Harvard Business Review.
4 *Small Is Beautiful: Economics as if People Mattered* (1973). Ernst F. Schumacher. Blond & Briggs.
5 'Wood wide web: trees' social networks are mapped' (15 May 2019). Claire Marshall. BBC https://www.bbc.co.uk/news/science-environment-48257315
6 'Open Innovation and the Triple Win'. Tom Winstanley. https://cxomag.com/open-innovation-and-the-triple-win
7 Net Zero Innovation Programme (NZIP). https://www.ucl.ac.uk/public-policy/home/collaborate/net-zero-innovation-programme
8 National Coordinating Centre for Public Engagement. https://www.publicengagement.ac.uk/about-engagement/why-does-public-engagement-matter
9 The Co-Production Collective. https://www.coproductioncollective.co.uk/
10 Net Zero Innovation Programme (NZIP) https://www.ucl.ac.uk/public-policy/net-zero-innovation-programme-ucl-and-local-government-association-collaboration

Chapter 5

1 "Understanding Leadership" Tom Marshall, Sovereign World International, 1991.
2 UCB Word for Today (26 May 2021). United Christian Broadcasters (UCB). https://www.ucb.co.uk/word-for-today/73500
3 'The Wright Brothers'. Wikipedia. https://en.wikipedia.org/wiki/Wright_brothers
4 'From transactional to transformative' (2018). Nik Miller. More Partnership, p 25.
5 'Environmental, Social and Corporate Governance'. Wikipedia. https://en.wikipedia.org/wiki/Environmental,_social_and_corporate_governance
6 'Will Covid-19 lead to more equitable research links?' (2 September 2020). Ellie Bothwell. *Times Higher Education.* https://www.timeshighereducation.com/world-university-rankings/will-covid-19-lead-more-equitable-research-links
7 CaSE has published a report in 2019, 'Building on Scientific strength: the next decade of R&D investment', on how the government can achieve this by 2027. https://www.sciencecampaign.org.uk/resource/nextdecade.html
8 'Learning for life: funding world class adult education' (2020). CBI. https://www.cbi.org.uk/articles/learning-for-life-funding-a-world-class-adult-education-system/
9 African Union Agenda 2063: https://au.int/agenda2063/sdgs

[10] African Union Continental Education for Africa. https://au.int/sites/default/files/documents/29958-doc-cesa_-_english-v9.pdf

[11] *Impact: Reshaping Capitalism to Drive Real Change* (2020) Ronald Cohen. Ebury Press.

[12] UK R&D Roadmap (July 2020). p 30. https://assets.publishing.service.gov.uk/government/uploads/system/uploads/attachment_data/file/896799/UK_Research_and_Development_Roadmap.pdf

[13] 'Understanding the immediate impacts of the Covid-19 crisis' (2020). Tomas Coates Ulrichsen. NCUB. https://www.ifm.eng.cam.ac.uk/uploads/UCI/knowledgehub/documents/2020_Ulrichsen_NCUBSoR2020_Covid_Universities.pdf

[14] Future Insight Prize. https://www.merckgroup.com/en/research/open-innovation/futureinsightprize_streaming.html

[15] The Earthshot Prize: https://earthshotprize.org/

[16] 'European Commission – Final Report of the High-Level Panel of the European Decarbonisation Pathways Initiative' (2018). Publication Office of the European Union. doi:10.2777/636. https://ec.europa.eu/info/publications/final-report-high-level-panel-european-decarbonisation-pathways-initiative_en

Index

References to figures appear in *italic* type;
those in **bold** type refer to tables.

F